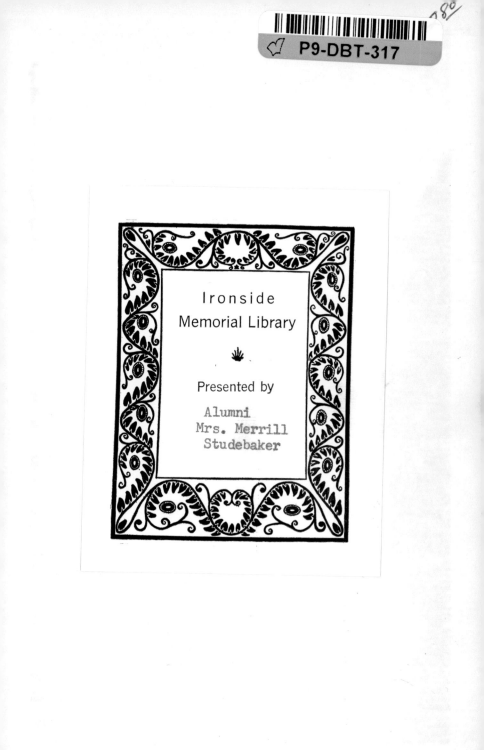

Crises in Morality

Crises in Morality

Edited by
C. W. SCUDDER

BROADMAN PRESS
Nashville, Tennessee

DEWEY DECIMAL CLASSIFICATION: 261.8
Library of Congress catalog card number: 64–18189
Printed in the United States of America
2.5MH65KSP

25979

Preface

The Christian minister is faced today with the necessity of dealing with many difficult social and ethical issues. Almost daily he is confronted by a wide range of problems in the lives of those to whom he ministers. Faced with the necessity for making moral judgments, both pastor and people are in need of reliable information and Christian insights.

Some of the issues which must be faced are of a distinctly controversial nature. However, all vital issues are really controversial. Harold A. Bosley has wisely said, "The only way to avoid controversial issues is to avoid vital issues. This the Christian preacher can scarcely afford to do." [1]

To better prepare preachers for the task ahead, we at Southwestern Baptist Theological Seminary for several years have offered a graduate seminar in which students do research concerning current ethical issues. This volume is the result of interest developed in the seminar. All of the contributors are former students who are now serving effectively in responsible places of Christian service. The thoughts and insights of these men, based upon their research, should prove to be profitable for pastors, and for all sincere Christians.

There are many facets to the difficult problem presented by current sexual immorality. Dealing with sexual matters has always been a

---

[1] *Preaching on Controversial Issues* (New York: Harper & Bros., 1953), p. 15.

difficult problem for the minister. Many sincere Christians still feel that sex is not a subject with which the preacher should deal. Dr. Julian Bridges has given a concise picture of the development of the present problem of sex morality in America, along with some practical advice to churches with regard to stemming the tide and changing the current of American immorality. There is a note of urgency in his challenge to the churches to undertake the task.

Many Christians feel that to help the unwed mother is to condone her sin and encourage continued laxity in sex morality. However, failure to help will continue to leave thousands of young girls, pregnant out of wedlock, at the mercy of those who will use their condition for selfish gain. Surely, the churches must seek the redemption of these young women both spiritually and socially. It is in the midst of dire need that people most readily turn to God. Much information, evaluation, and practical counsel is crowded into chapter 2.

Perhaps no social problem with which the Christian minister is faced produces within him a more helpless feeling than does the problem of perverted sex. So pastors will welcome the evaluation and information contained in chapter 3. Technical terminology has been kept at a minimum in an effort to provide practical help.

There are many vital issues in the area of life and death. Three of the most pressing problems are considered in Part II. The present population explosion is the background for the present controversy concerning birth control. However, it is the more personal considerations with regard to the will of God to which Dr. James Robinson gives attention in chapter 4. The author limits himself to the problem which is central for the Christian: Is it right or wrong? He clearly sets forth the pastoral approach in helping people make a moral decision.

As he ministers to the incurably ill and their families, the Christian minister can hardly avoid dealing with the matter of mercy killing. Dr. Yates Bingham, an Air Force chaplain, limits himself to consideration of voluntary euthanasia. He sets forth the differing views concerning the subject and also gives his own evaluation and conclusions. A widespread knowledge of the subject is needed as continued efforts are put forth in seeking the legalization of euthanasia.

Capital punishment is the problem with which chapter 6 deals. Current controversy has heightened the need for a Christian evaluation of the practice. Although many may not agree with all of Dr. Huey's conclusions, a careful reading of this chapter should result in the establishing and strengthening of Christian convictions. The author holds that to simply acquiesce in present practices is to commit murder by proxy every time a criminal is executed. This concise treatment of the subject clarifies the central issue.

There are many difficult and significant problems in human relations today. Three are given attention in Part III. The race problem in America is analyzed from a Christian perspective in chapter 7. This brief treatment of a big problem should sensitize the Christian conscience and challenge to Christian action.

Chapter 8 gets beyond mere consideration of Communist ideology and deals with the effects of the Communist program in the realm of human relations. Here is real help in understanding and meeting the Communist challenge to Christianity.

A problem which merits much more attention is considered in the final chapter. Mind-poisoning and the prostituting of emotions through the mass media of communication continues almost unhindered today. Many consciences are troubled concerning the matter of censorship and freedom. Can the conflict between the two be reconciled? This chapter should help to clarify the issues involved. Action should be based upon well-informed convictions.

Limited space allowed for each of these subjects has made a thorough treatment impossible. However, the suggested reading at the close of each chapter will provide guidance in more thorough study and consideration.

Although not agreeing fully with every statement and every emphasis contained in the following chapters, I do believe that both the information they contain and the insights that they share should produce great profit for the cause of Christ in a day of social tension and crisis.

C. W. SCUDDER

Contents

1
America's Problem
of Sex Morality

JULIAN C. BRIDGES

A group of young people had gathered in the church fellowship hall for an informal discussion on love, courtship, and marriage. The expression on their faces indicated intense interest in the subject under discussion. There was a look of earnestness and anticipation as they waited for an answer to the question just read. The pastor who led the group reread the words written on the slip of paper submitted to him: "What is wrong with a sincere couple having sex relations before marriage?"

Is it rather startling that such a question would be asked in a group of church young people, the majority of whom are Christians? This and similar questions concerning sexual morality are being asked by thousands of youths across America. The dean of one large university reports that one of the questions most frequently asked among his students is "why sex relations before marriage are not moral." [1] If you were in the place of the pastor or the dean, what would your answer be? One thing is certain—young people want to know, and they must know if they are to uphold Christian standards of morality. Youths of today are confused by the fact that many people seem to feel that Christian standards of sexual morality are only pious proclamations and have no practical relevance to personal morality.

Confusion and uncertainty are not limited to the youth of America. In fact, one reason for the frequency with which questions on sexual

---

[1] Sylvanus M. Duvall, *Men, Women and Morals* (New York: Association Press, 1952), p. 5.

morality arise in youth meetings is that their elders are likewise confused about what is ethical. Three examples taken from the files of a well-known author and marriage consultant illustrate this fact.[2] The first concerns a mother who states that her daughter is terribly in love with a boy about her own age. The mother and father realize that the romance will probably not last long. In the meantime, however, the mother feels that the youths are under a terrific strain. She wants to know if it would not be better for her to take her daughter to a gynecologist, have her fitted with a diaphragm, and then allow the young people to have relations in the parents' home under supervision.

A second case is that of a woman who says that her sex drive is at its height just as that of her husband, ten years older, is diminishing. Her question is, if her husband is no longer able to satisfy her, why should she not establish some relationships with other men, provided she is discreet and careful?

The above two counselees may not be Christians and perhaps are somewhat the exception; they are, nonetheless, cited as representative of countless adults who are asking similar questions. Neither should it be concluded that Christians are not confused about the matter of sexual morality today. Duvall's third example should eliminate any doubt that church people also need guidance in clarifying their thinking about sexual morality. A pastor said that while formerly in the navy chaplaincy he became "broad-minded" about sex. He didn't object when his wife wanted relations with men other than himself. Now, however, he is in the pastorate, and if she continues to act as she does, it will ruin him vocationally. His question is, shouldn't his wife have some consideration for his work if it means so much to him?

These examples reflect the urgent need for Christian leaders and churches to develop some adequate answers to the pressing problems which confront people in the area of sex morality. Such situations also illustrate the fact that the discussion of the subject of sex is no longer taboo. American people are much less puritanical than they once were. Sex in one form or another is displayed and discussed on every hand—on billboards, over television, in newspapers, and on the street corner. American culture has become supersaturated with sex!

---

[2] *Ibid.*

In the midst of what the eminent Harvard sociologist Pitirim Sorokin has called "the American sex revolution," there exists a tremendous spiritual vacuum. This dearth of spiritual discernment has led to moral confusion, which is widespread. The alarming fact is that sexual immorality continues to increase at a tremendous rate.

What can be done to curb and combat the menace of increasing sexual immorality? This is the searching question confronting all conscientious Christians. In order to adequately answer it, something must be seen of the background and development of sexual morality in America. Only as an understanding of the development of the sex code is acquired can the present problems be properly evaluated and a workable solution proposed.

Historical Development

How did the present attitude of looseness in sexual morality develop? Actually, the history of American sexual morality may be divided into two major periods—the time of the older sex code and the time of transition.

The older sex code.—What does it mean to refer to the sex code of the "old order"? Historically, the period covers the time from the passing of the "frontier" until the time of World War I. Morally, the code of this period can simply be stated as forbidding sexual intercourse outside of marriage and sanctioning it within marriage. However, such a brief statement does not suffice in giving an understanding of morality for the period. It is necessary to know what the older code was designed to do and also something of what made it work.

The purposes of the code were several. A primary purpose was to continue Christian ideals by upholding the teachings of the Bible, which forbid any sexual relationship outside of marriage. The influence of Christianity on the sex standards of secular society was unmistakably powerful at this time.

A second purpose of the older sex code was to preserve family life. It was important to society that each child born should have parents who both acknowledged and assumed responsibility for him. Preventing irresponsible pregnancies was thus a social as well as an individual obligation. During this period, the family was the unit of economic production and the usual means to economic power and social position.

Still another practical purpose of the code was to assure male domination. This was true in the wider areas of economic, political, and social life, as well as in the sexual realm. The woman's place was in the home with the children, while the man was expected to handle the affairs of the world outside the home.

The question might well be asked as to how effective these provisions and restrictions were in maintaining sexual standards of purity. On the whole they were surprisingly effective. A sizable minority of men lived up fairly well to the ideal. They refrained from sex relationships outside of marriage and sought to eliminate sex thoughts and feelings from their lives. As for the majority, the studies of Kinsey and others indicate that the power of the sex urge was influenced by the use of the "dirty story" and constant group pressure. Yet, even among the majority, sex taboos had significant effects. Most men accepted them as valid and felt guilty when they violated them. Furthermore, a large portion of those who even habitually had illicit relations would not approach respectable women and girls.

For these men society allowed other outlets that were less generally accepted. Unofficially, a large proportion of society, most men and many women, approved the discussion of sex through the "dirty story." Another outlet was provided by the "double standard of morality." If men respected decent women, many felt they should be free to approach the "other kind." Such conclusions were bitterly opposed from certain quarters; yet, there was enough social demand for permitting men to have sexual outlets outside of marriage that prostitution was recognized as part of the older sex code.

In summary, then, it should be said that the sex code of the past was a practical arrangement designed to meet definite objectives, which were important to the people of those times. A primary purpose was to prevent illicit sex relations with respectable women and girls. Taboos were supported and enforced because they were held to be functionally necessary. The survival of those taboos which have endured until today will, likewise, probably depend on whether people feel that they accomplish something which needs to be done.

The time of transition.—It is now important to consider what happened to the older sex code and its system of supporting taboos. The time of transition noticeably began with World War I and continues until today. It is the bridge between the sex code of the old order and the sex revolution which is still in progress in America.

The nature of the transition period is seen first in the breakdown of the old discussion taboos. As early as 1905, attempts at "sex education" were made in a very mild form. About this time, people were becoming increasingly aware of the problem of prostitution. Discussion of this "social evil" with carefully chosen words was often regarded as not only proper but a civic and religious duty as well.

The change from the "hush-hush" attitude toward sex began for very necessary reasons. Increasingly, the conviction grew that young people, and even children, should have an adequate understanding of the facts of life rather than confused thinking accumulated from superstitions and stories picked up from companions.

Discussions of sex, however, were not long to be limited to idealistic educational objectives. "As the corrupt trader often follows the missionary, so selfish vested interests took advantage of the freedom won by idealists to exploit sex commercially." [3] Writers of fiction proceeded cautiously at first. They met the requirements of modesty, but at the same time they often made the subject more alluring. The dissolution of taboos on modesty closely followed the elimination of those concerning discussion of sex.

It was not until the beginning of World War I that women's ankles made their first appearances. Gradually but steadily the feminine hemline grew higher. When women entered sports, particularly tennis and swimming, their apparel became increasingly abbreviated. Modesty taboos did not disappear all at once, however, for some taboos still remain today. But the grip of modesty without a doubt was broken.

The main result of the transition in sexual morality has not been a change in particular practices but a complete reversal of whole social attitudes toward sex. Most Americans in the past regarded sex as something that could neither be rejected nor acknowledged. Adult mates found in it a shameful but delightful companion. What caused such profound changes in the attitude toward sex? Not one thing but a combination of things.

Since the old conduct restrictions had particular application to women, any change in the status of womanhood naturally affected them greatly. Increased economic opportunities for women in recent

---

[3] *Ibid.*, p. 19.

years have had much to do with sex morality. A woman who could work outside the home no longer had to marry unless she wanted to. Thus, if she practiced conduct which would make her socially unacceptable as a wife, she at least did not have to starve. Likewise, a woman no longer had to live at home with her family unless she chose to do so. She could go to another city if she wished. In the larger city no one would know who she was or what she did. She would be comparatively free of the chaperonage of both community and family. With the arrival of the automobile, she could quickly get where no one knew her, even if she lived in the country.

Another of the most important factors in giving women a feeling of security from detection was improved methods of birth control. Though she still cannot have absolute safety, she is safe enough that she may dare to take the risk if she chooses to do so. It is difficult to state just how influential birth control methods have been in eliminating fear of pregnancy.

Still another factor is that a new knowledge of the nature of personality was fostered by the eminent psychologist Sigmund Freud. Freud's conclusions do not need to be endorsed to recognize that he has thrown a flood of light upon the basic needs and motivations of people. The resulting insights have profoundly influenced people's attitudes toward the place and legitimacy of sex needs. Social pathology and cultural anthropology have also made significant contributions toward understanding the human personality and rightly relating sex to life.

Again, twice within a generation, millions of men have been withdrawn from ordinary civilian life and subjected to conditions under which the usual concerns and controls were absent. War always challenges moral standards and it seems that sex delinquency is one of its most familiar accompaniments.

It is only necessary to mention that while the sex code of the past was designed to support family solidarity, such solidarity is almost no longer existent in millions of homes across America. For many people such protection for the family no longer seems necessary. However mistaken people may be, their feelings have been significant in weakening the supporting sex code.

Commercial enterprises have capitalized on the shifting standards of the older code. They have found gold in sex, not only through prostitution, but through salacious literature, movies, advertising, and almost every other medium of public communication. Thus, the greed for money has led many to exploit this situation of a changing sex code for economic advantage. As a consequence, sex has so preoccupied our civilization that it now oozes from all pores of American life.

In addition to the above, the rise of hedonistic philosophy, increased consumption of alcoholic beverages, a decline of moral and religious training in the home, and intimate relations caused by crowded housing conditions are a few other factors which have contributed to the breakdown of the old sexual standards of morality.

Present Practice

What has been the result of this rapid transition from the older sex code to the sex revolution of today?

A college girl in a class on human behavior in a Pennsylvania school stood up to answer a professor's question on the role of sex in life. "Sex is like raw meat," she said, "when you're hungry you take it." It is sex freedom that has been proclaimed as the great emancipator of a restricted mankind, and morality has been seen as a confining dungeon. Especially since the close of World War II, there has been a campaign for sex "liberation." Men, women, and adolescents were to be freed of the inhibitions of an outdated morality. Human emotions were to be released from their dungeon of gloom and shadows by the sun of science by day and the stars of statistics by night. Thus, stone by stone, the confining dungeon has been torn away. But Americans should look around and see if it is actually a dungeon being torn away or the very homes in which they live.

Disintegration of family life.—Marriage itself has been seen by the sex liberators as a social custom much too rigid for modern times. The notion of a husband and wife's remaining loyal and in love until death parts them is ridiculed as outmoded morality. But what prizes has such a notion won America?

In 1867, when the first reliable statistics on divorce in the United States were gathered, there was a rate of 0.3 divorces per thousand population. In 1962, the rate had grown to 2.2 divorces per thousand population. In 1870, there was one divorce for every 33.7 marriages contracted, and in the last few years, one for about every 3.5. According to Sorokin, the United States leads all Europe and the Americas in divorce rate (having three times the rate of France, four times that of England, six times that of Canada, and eight times that of Mexico).[4]

Similar increase is noted in the number of desertions or the "poor man's divorce." According to the National Desertion Bureau, desertion cost the American taxpayer, in 1953, about 252 million dollars for the support of abandoned wives and children. About three and one-half million children receive annually little or no financial aid from the father. As a result of this mounting number of divorces, separations, and desertions, about 12 million of the 45 million children in the United States do not live with both parents. Can sex freedom justify these statistics?

The above facts indicate an increasing incapacity for harmonious relations within the home. And since the "marriage-family school" increasingly fails to graduate socially well-adjusted and mature individuals, the nation and ultimately mankind are bound to be made up more and more of individuals less and less capable of getting along with one another.

Another indication of the disintegration of family life is seen in the growing practice of premarital intercourse. How many people today engage in such a practice at least once before they marry if they do marry? The most complete and most recent statistics for answering this question are found in the studies of Indiana University under the direction of the late Alfred C. Kinsey. Though his conclusions have proved to be quite controversial, his discoveries do give some line of direction. Kinsey reported that 98 per cent of the men who never go beyond grade school engage in premarital intercourse at some time. For those who never go beyond high school, 84 per cent have the experience; and for those who go to college, 67 per cent.[5]

In relation to religious background, sexual behavior was considerably lower for active and devout men than for inactive or less devout. But there is no evidence to show that interest in religion inhibits interest in sex. It is the kind and degree of interest in religion which seems to have influence on sexual activity.

The situation for women appears on the surface to be quite different, for only 30 per cent of the grade school group had

---

[4] Pitirim A. Sorokin, *The American Sex Revolution* (Boston: Porter Sargent Publisher, 1956), p. 8.

[5] Alfred C. Kinsey *et al., Sexual Behavior in the Human Male* (Philadelphia: W. B. Saunders Co., 1948), p. 552.

premarital relations and 47 per cent of the high school group, while the figure for the college women was 60 per cent. Nearly 50 per cent of the total had had intercourse before marriage. It should be mentioned that a considerable number of these had such relations only with their fiancés just before marriage.[6]

In relation to religious background there is for women a definite correlation between interest and activity in the church and lower rates of total sexual activity, with the possible exception of sex relations practiced within marriage. Among the devout, only 24 to 30 per cent stated they had sex relations; whereas, among the less devout, 55 to 63 per cent acknowledged their experience.

Still a more serious factor in the breakdown of the American home is the growing practice of extramarital intercourse. Most people feel that marital infidelity will not happen in their marriage, but facts prove it can happen to almost anyone—the normal as well as the neurotic, the happily married as well as those who are not happy. Frank Caprio has pointed out that all are "potentially susceptible to give expression to . . . polygamous inclinations." [7]

Kinsey concluded that it is probably safe to suggest that about 50 per cent of all the married males have intercourse with women other than their wives at some time while they are married. Among women, there are probably about 26 per cent who have extramarital relations by age forty, according to Kinsey.

If Kinsey's studies are accepted as even relatively correct, they paint a very dark picture of the sex morals of American men and women. To be sure, the Kinsey reports do not have to be read to recognize that irregularity and illicit sexual behavior is more prevalent today than at any time in the history of the United States.

Illegitimacy on the increase.—According to data from recent reports of the United States Public Health Service, illegitimate births have reached an all-time high. The annual total for 1963 lists 240,200 births out of wedlock. The mothers of 41 per cent of these babies are teen-agers. In a Cleveland hospital 176 cases of illegitimacy were traced and tabulated by a juvenile judge. He found the average age of the mothers to be fourteen years and six months.

Closely related to illegitimacy is the problem of abortions. Sorokin

---

[6] Alfred C. Kinsey, *Sexual Behavior in the Human Female* (Philadelphia: W. B. Saunders Co., 1953), p. 276.

[7] *Marital Infidelity* (New York: Citadel Press, 1953), p. 3.

says that the number of abortions (performed most frequently for unwed girls or sinning wives) is estimated at the astonishing figure of between 333,000 and 1,000,000 annually.

Prostitution and disease.—The number of prostitutes in the United States cannot be adequately determined, but the *Encyclopedia Americana* estimates that in the mid 1940s there were approximately six hundred thousand. Kinsey reported that some 60 per cent of the total white male population ultimately has some experience with prostitutes. It is estimated that from one-half to one billion dollars are received per year from the practice of prostitution.

The prevalence of venereal disease is closely related to the practice of prostitution. Syphilis rates rose in 1956 for the first time since 1948. They finally caught up with the miracle antibiotics, which were to be the secret defense for sex freedom. However, the American Social Hygiene Association reports that VD rates are rising. Control programs are inadequate. Between eighty and one hundred thousand new cases were reported in the United States in 1963. One out of every six reported was in the fifteen- to nineteen-year-old age group.

Trends in marital morality.—It is important to observe not only present conditions but also trends, especially with reference to marital morality. Whenever sex is misused, either before or after marriage, God's highest purposes are thwarted and marital unhappiness results.

Sorokin laments the present sad state of affairs with reference to sexual morality: "If the present rate of decline of premarital virginity continues, this virtue is likely to become within a few generations a myth of the past." [8] Other authorities such as Kinsey and Lewis Terman agree. Kinsey feels that the major change during the past three decades has been in the conduct of women. What was once the double standard of morality seems now to have become the single standard of immorality. Every technical study shows that the proportion of women who observe the older standards has declined in recent years. Terman found that the percentage of women who were virgins at the time of marriage was 86.5 per cent for those born before 1890, but only 31.7 per cent for those born after 1910. [9] He concludes that virginity will be close to the vanishing point for women born after 1940, if the present trend continues.

---

[8] *Op. cit.,* p. 14.

[9] Lewis M. Terman, *Psychological Factors in Marital Happiness* (New York: McGraw-Hill Book Co., 1938), pp. 321 ff.

In the matter of extramarital relations there is also substantial increase among women. Of the married women born before 1900, only 22 per cent had had extramarital intercourse by the age of forty. But of the women born between 1900 and 1910, 30 per cent had such relations by the same age.[10]

Conclusion.—The older sex code surely has undergone significant changes, many of which seem to be permanent. On the other hand, there is no indication that the ideal for restricting intercourse to marriage will be changed in the foreseeable future. As a consequence, America's children grow up in a society where sex is a social concern but to which private indulgence is given. Americans are actually living a life of hypocrisy, since they acknowledge one code but practice as they please. What can be done about it all? Surely, the church can make significant contributions to the code and the conduct of American people.

Christian Contribution

What can the Christian churches do to stem the tide and change the current of immorality? Surely, they cannot sit idly by and see America continue to drift toward sexual anarchy. This nation's only hope lies in a revitalized Christianity, awake and alert to the needs of society today. Though the older sex code is almost obliterated, can there not be constructed upon it a new code which is both practical and Christian in content? If so, what must the church do to bring such a code into existence and into wide acceptance?

Relation of religion to sex morality.—Some people both within and without the church would feel better if the subject of sex could be excluded from religion altogether. Those on the outside do not like the dogmatic, moralistic attitudes which religious leaders sometimes take. Those on the inside still feel that sex is "shameful" and "naughty" and should not be discussed. However, religious influences have a tremendous effect upon sex conduct. A discussion of sex morals which omits religion would be mutilated and distorted.

There is a great need for the church to state its sexual ethic in terms which everyone can understand. The social control that the church has tried to exercise has been done mainly through reliance upon

[10] Seward Hiltner, "The Past and Present," *Sexual Behavior in American Society*, eds. Jerome Himelhoch and Sylvia Fleis Fava (New York: W. W. Norton Co., 1955), p. 314.

intangible concepts. The difficulty is that many churches have done nothing to help those, young and old, who are struggling with moral decisions. Young people and adults need a demonstration and an attitude on the part of their spiritual leaders and pastors of acceptance of the plain facts of sex and of its rightful purposes and meanings.

A pastor and his people have a unique opportunity and responsibility to lead others to a saving relationship with a God of love; God in turn wants to help his own with their problems of love, both physical and spiritual. He is the author of all genuine love, and he seeks to solve those difficulties which may arise in the hearts of his children.

Religion is urgently needed to serve as the integrating force between sex solely on the physical plane and all that Christ conceives true marriage to be. It must be remembered that "it is not sexual behavior that determines character; it is character that determines sexual behavior." [11] Sex is not in its proper use as an end in itself. Thus, the motives of sex behavior are the most important matters, and this is where Christianity can exert its most powerful influence. The great need today, then, is for the churches to awaken to their opportunities for exerting influences which can greatly change the sexual conduct of America. It is important to view the means accessible to the church for this objective.

Means of influencing sexual morality.—What methods are available for a local church to use in effecting a change in the sexual morality of its members, its community, and its nation? First, the churches can see that their members are informed concerning current sexual morality. Many are not fully aware that the moral practices of the American people have grown worse in the last fifteen years. Definite avenues of approach are available for educating and making practical the Christian interpretation of sex.

The pulpit provides one of the best opportunities for dealing with the issues of sex morality. The pastor should avail himself of the opportunity to preach special messages on the Christian home, either as occasional sermons or in a series. An added emphasis may be given by making incidental references to and illustrations of sexual morality and the Christian ideal for conduct in this realm. Preaching offers a medium for expressing his attitudes toward the subject of sex. In this

---

[11] Joseph Fletcher, "A Moral Philosophy of Sex," *Sex and Religion Today,* ed. Simon Doniger (New York: Association Press, 1953), p. 192.

way he can build confidence among his people, which will encourage them to seek his counsel more often. An indication of genuine concern for helping people to solve sexual problems will bring many a needy church member to the pastor's study for advice.

One of the richest resources available for pastors and church workers is in the field of counseling. By casual contacts, home visitation, and a definite time set aside in his schedule, the pastor can meet the needs and solve the problems of many of his members. In the premarital conference he may also place into the hands of the couple he is soon to marry helpful materials dealing with the sexual side of marriage.

The church organizations provide a worthwhile outlet for helping church members meet their problems. The teachers and leaders who work with the various organizations can accomplish much good by dealing frankly and forcefully with the issues at stake. The church's position on premarital and extramarital intercourse should be clearly and affirmatively stated. One needs to know God's design for the home and the right use of sex. A youth should know how to best prepare for Christian marriage. Parents must be encouraged to train their children concerning the divine purpose of sex and not leave this for someone else to do.

There should be an honest, open approach to the subject of sex with a positive emphasis on clean, moral living. Study course books should be utilized in planning a week of emphasis on the Christian home. Other helpful literature such as a Christian family magazine should be made available to every home in the church membership.

The church library can become a source of real help both to the married and to those who are single. Names of publications and source material on all matters pertaining to marriage and sex are usually available from the church's denominational headquarters. By appropriating a small percentage of its funds for the purchase of the best books on the subject, the church library can be a storehouse of information.

Many situations involving people with sexual problems are too serious to be handled by the amateur counselor. Such persons need professional assistance or at least adequate literature prepared by professional people. In many communities there are agencies already established to give aid to those with such problems. The church library can render real service if it lists these agencies with the kind of assistance offered, the names and addresses of the officials, and the conditions under which they are ready to respond. Individuals needing help do not have to stumble along in guesswork as long as trained counselors are available.

Numerous opportunities for discussion-group counseling, and instruction on the issues of sexual morality are possible through special conferences. Sunday evening fellowship hours are especially appealing to young people. Parent-teacher conferences may be advantageous.

The church can lead in inspiring community-wide projects which will provide a more wholesome atmosphere for sexual morality. This calls for co-operating with parent-teacher associations, civic groups, and other churches. Surely, there will be co-operative effort on such an important matter. By inspiring the parents of the community with a genuine interest and spirit of willingness to help, many homes will be better informed as to how to instruct their children in matters pertaining to sex.

The church can also supply opportunities to form deep, abiding friendships. The importance of a couple's friends is recognized by the students of marriage. The couples with the highest marriage adjustment, in the Burgess and Cottrell studies, were most numerous among "those of which each partner had many friends of the same sex and a few—but not too many—of the opposite sex." [12] The Bible urges hospitality and friendship. Christians are admonished to be "fervent in your love among yourselves; . . . using hospitality one to another" (1 Peter 4:8–9, ASV).

Conclusion.—The church can be a potent force in establishing the new code of sexual morality. Failure of the divine institution to use its influence for positive action in this area of morality today could result in sexual anarchy. Through the means mentioned above, the church can go far toward combating the trend toward increased sexual immorality. In order to do this it must be better informed about the facts, be more explicit about what it believes, and avail itself of the numerous opportunities to help those in need. America and the world await Christians and churches who will be courageous and uncompromising in their stand against immorality, while adopting a positive Christian program for a new moral code built upon the biblical teachings concerning sex.

---

[12] Ray E. Baber, *Marriage and the Family* (2d ed.; New York: McGraw-Hill Book Co., 1953), p. 157.

Sex is dynamite! Unchallenged by Christian character, it leads to chaos and destruction. It can be the strongest tie that binds, but it can also be the lever that pries people apart. The danger is that while medical and industrial technology has made intercourse easier, moral ability to uphold ideals has not kept pace. Sex, then, is not a scientific but a religious and moral problem for this age. It is much like the new nuclear energy—science can make it more readily accessible, but man must decide what end such power shall accomplish. Every Christian has an all-important part to play.

Suggested Reading [13]

COLE, WILLIAM GRAHAM. *Sex and Love in the Bible*. New York, Association Press, 1959.

DONIGER, SIMON (ed.). *Sex and Religion Today*. New York: Association Press, 1953. Written from the viewpoint of pastoral psychology based upon the relation of sex to religion.

HILTNER, SEWARD. *Sex and the Christian Life*. New York: Association Press, 1957. A Christian view of sex compared and contrasted to other prevalent contemporary views.

HIMELHOCH, JEROME, and FAVA, SYLVIA FLEIS (eds.). *Sexual Behavior in American Society*. New York: W. W. Norton Co., 1955. A practical and factual summary and appraisal of the first two Kinsey reports edited for the Society for the Study of Social Problems.

---

[13] In addition to those sources cited in the chapter, the following are recommended.

2

Mothers Out of Wedlock

BILL PINSON

"I'm going to have a baby!" The pastor remembered the many times he had heard these words· from happy mothers-to-be. But the girl sitting across from his desk sobbed hysterically as she cried over and over again, "I'm going to have a baby! What am I going to do?"

A bright student, a charming personality, a beautiful teen-ager, a long-time church member—pregnant out of wedlock. Now she would be known as *that* girl.

Many questions swirled through the pastor's mind: How could this happen? How many other girls are in such trouble? What can be done to help her? What can be done to help others avoid such tragedy? The following pages are devoted to discovering the answers to questions such as these.

Realizing the Problem

Few people are concerned about the problem of unwed mothers. Several factors contribute to this unconcern. A cloak of secrecy usually surrounds the unwed mother and, therefore, little is known about her. Also, the agencies which work with unwed mothers have too long operated behind closed doors. Concern can grow only where there is knowledge. When people realize the extensiveness of the problem, they usually become concerned.

Because of the nature of the problem, accurate statistics concerning its extent are difficult to gather. A conservative estimate is that 4 per cent of the total births in the United States are to unwed mothers; the number of such births reported each year is now approximately two hundred thousand. The known births do not tell the whole story.

Marriages after conception, unrecorded births, infanticides, and abortions are numerous, but they do not figure into the statistics.

This has been a growing problem. The national office of vital statistics indicates that in 1938 there were 88,000 out-of-wedlock births and that in 1961 there were 240,200. During the past two decades there has been a 120 per cent increase.

The harmful effect of the problem on individuals and on society is very great. The girl who is pregnant out of wedlock usually suffers physical and emotional harm, social ostracism, alienation from the love and affection of parents and friends; and, if she is an adolescent, interruption or termination of her education. In some instances the teen-age girl is liable to a charge in juvenile court as a delinquent. If adequate guidance and help are not supplied, she may turn to prostitution.

The unwed father is also affected. He usually assumes or is legally forced to assume financial support for the mother and child. Frequently he suffers emotional harm. His career may be ruined and, if he is already married, his marriage may be broken by the incident.

The parents frequently suffer an emotional shock and a loss of status in the community. The girl's parents often must bear the medical costs; and, if the girl decides to keep her child, they usually contribute to his support.

The children born out of wedlock, who are in no way responsible, suffer more than anyone else. In many states they must bear a social and legal stigma. Often they have unusual emotional difficulties and adjustments. If they discover the circumstances of their birth, they may develop a psychological bent toward out-of-wedlock pregnancy.

Children born out of wedlock are often a burden to society. Frequently they are maladjusted and, therefore, are a disruptive factor. The cost of their support is heavy. One writer has indicated that it is costing the taxpayers approximately 210 million dollars a year to support more than 300,000 illegitimate children.[1]

Certain rackets are also fostered. One of the most heartless, the black market for babies, depends on out-of-wedlock births for its existence. Doctors who perform illegal abortions charge exorbitant fees. Blackmail and unjust paternity suits are other undesirable practices made possible by such pregnancies.

---

[1] "Pregnancies Grow in Washington Schools," *U.S. News and World Report*, XLIII (July 12, 1957), 66.

In addition to the extent and effect of the problem, its complexity must also be realized. The problem of unwed mothers is not a simple one. A strictly moralistic approach is inadequate. The problem has religious, social, economic, and psychological implications.

Understanding the Unwed Mother

The unmarried mother fits into no particular category. All authorities agree that there is no typical case. For example, all possible types of marital status are represented among those pregnant out of wedlock: married, divorced, separated, widowed, and unmarried.

All economic, social, and racial groups are represented. However, where poverty is combined with any degree of social disorganization, such as slum or isolated rural areas, the number of out-of-wedlock pregnancies is higher than in other areas. Among Negroes, who on the whole usually suffer a greater degree of poverty and social disorganization than white citizens, the proportion of out-of-wedlock births is higher than among whites.

All religious groups are represented. The majority of unwed mothers claims affiliation with some religious group. Some are vocational Christian workers. Others profess to having had deep spiritual experiences.

All ages, from puberty to menopause, are represented. However, the vast majority of out-of-wedlock pregnancies occurs among young women and adolescent girls. Approximately 70 per cent of the known unmarried mothers are under twenty-five years of age and approximately 50 per cent are in adolescence. On the other hand, most homes for unwed mothers report that every year they care for some women who are over forty.

All levels of education are represented. Approximately 50 per cent have a high school education or more. A few, probably less than 5 per cent, have a college education or more. Also, all types of vocations are represented. However, the groups most heavily represented are students and office workers. The large number of unwed mothers who are students can be attributed to the fact that the majority is in the student age group.

All types of personality structures and temperaments are represented among unwed mothers. However, the general types of persons who tend to engage in sexual intercourse outside of marriage, and are thus vulnerable to out-of-wedlock pregnancy, are the following: (1)

The unconventional person with few or no religious roots; (2) the underprivileged person socially or economically; (3) the person who has a need for love at all costs; (4) the rebellious youngster who indulges sexually just to prove to someone that she can; and (5) the couple deeply involved in romance who for some reason cannot marry.[2] The so-called "bad" girl seldom becomes pregnant out of wedlock because she is careful to avoid it.

The causes of the problem are complex. No simple answer can be given to the question, "Why does it happen?" A number of wrong answers has been suggested. For example, it has been falsely reasoned that aid to dependent children causes women to become pregnant out of wedlock in order to receive the aid money. No sane woman, however, would go through the anguish of such an experience for the mere pittance of an aid-to-dependent-children check. Another suggestion is that humane treatment of unwed mothers encourages out-of-wedlock pregnancy. Actually, clinical and statistical studies indicate that the converse is true: poor care of unwed mothers frequently leads to a second such pregnancy. The Victorian concept that an out-of-wedlock pregnancy is the result of the seduction of an innocent maiden by an experienced blackguard just does not hold up under the weight of facts gathered from case studies.

The immediate cause of pregnancy out of wedlock is the decision by the girl to indulge in sexual intercourse with a man who is not her husband. In spite of all outside influences, in almost every case the girl is responsible for her act. There are exceptions, of course, such as in the case of rape, ignorance, mental illness, or extreme physiological disorder.

The physical cause is impregnation. This is the result of natural biological processes which occur when a contraceptive device fails or is not used. A large percentage of pregnancies out of wedlock is the result of failure to use preventive measures. Couples fail to use contraceptives because of ignorance, a sense of guilt, religious scruples, or a spontaneous sexual experience.

The primary causes are largely psychological and social. Those who work with unwed mothers agree that each girl's trouble can be traced to emotional and psychological difficulties created by circumstances in her life. Actually, her pregnancy is a symptom of an underlying

---

[2] Evelyn Duvall, "Premarital Sex—The Counselor's Challenge," *Pastoral Psychology,* X (December, 1959), 26–27.

problem which makes it difficult for the girl to control her biological impulses.

The psychological and emotional disorders assume various forms. Many unmarried mothers are neurotic and some are psychotic. Some are motivated by spite for parents or for self, others by jealousy of a friend or sister who is pregnant within the bonds of marriage. It is the thesis of Leontine Young in *Out of Wedlock* that numerous unwed mothers are driven by a subconscious desire for a baby, specifically an out-of-wedlock baby.

Several factors seem to contribute to the psychological and emotional difficulties which are a primary cause. The factor most frequently cited by these who work with unwed mothers is poor home life. Faulty parental relations contribute to emotional disturbances. Parental control is frequently either too lax or too strict. Problems are also created by broken homes. A lack of love in the home intensifies the desire to find love elsewhere.

Times of crisis often create emotional disturbances which precipitate sexual adventures that may lead to pregnancy. Examples of such crises are the marriage of a brother or sister, leaving home for school or work, the death of a parent or a dearly loved friend. Also, physical deformity or an unattractive appearance may lead to a dangerous emotional disorder. Such a girl may resort to promiscuity to gain affection or may yield herself fully to any man who shows any desire for her. Actually, the entire life pattern contributes to personality formation and each person must be looked upon as an individual to discover the factors which created a tendency to nonconformity in sexual behavior.

Social factors as well as personality disorders are involved in the out-of-wedlock pregnancy. The presence or absence of these social factors will frequently determine whether or not a girl with a personality disorder will yield to sexual activity outside of marriage. Also, certain of these social factors may contribute to personality disorder.

According to sociologists and doctors who have carefully studied the problem, the loose attitude toward sex, the removal of sexual restrictions, and nonconformist teachings on sex are contributing causes of pregnancy out of wedlock. So, too, are the communication and entertainment media which glorify and stimulate sexual passion.

Certain dating practices of young people stimulate sexual passion and thereby make out-of-bounds sexual activity more likely. Among these practices are petting, dancing, and listening to sensuous music. Also, certain factors, such as automobiles and motels, make possible a great deal of freedom in sexual activity. The use of liquor and narcotics and the influence of gangs and delinquent companions tend to cause a lowering of moral standards. There is evidence that the discussing of sexual experience by teen-age married couples with single friends encourages premarital sexual experience.

Neglect is also a cause of out-of-wedlock pregnancy—neglect by homes, by churches, by communities. Churches frequently fail to provide adequate relevant religious training and fail to lead members to dedication to Christ as Lord of life as well as Saviour of soul. Communities frequently fail to provide adequate recreational facilities and a wholesome community environment. The neglect of children by their parents has become a national disgrace in the United States.

Whatever the cause, an out-of-wedlock pregnancy is a trying experience for a girl. The reactions differ according to the personality of the girl involved, but certain reactions are common among unwed mothers. The woman pregnant out of wedlock suffers despair and loneliness. A feeling of helplessness, coupled with that of severe guilt, sometimes leads to suicide. Denial and a desire for concealment are frequent first reactions; this is dangerous because a lack of proper care may be the consequence.

The girl has three alternatives: marriage, abortion, or a child born out of wedlock. The present trend, according to available statistics, is away from forced marriage. Of course, if there is a desire for marriage by both parties, marriage may well prove to be the best course of action. Abortion is a frequent practice; it has been estimated that there are at least two abortions for each live birth out of wedlock.[3] The girl who decides to give birth to her baby must make many varied and important decisions, such as where to go, what to do about the man responsible, and what to do with the baby.

A desire for secrecy frequently leads to an attempt to get away from home. Many girls, however, remain at home throughout their pregnancy because they do not know anywhere else to go. In many cases it is not good for the girl to remain at home because this is the home that produced the unwed mother in the first place. The unwed mothers who

---

[3] Henry A. Bowman, *Marriage for Moderns* (4th ed.; New York: McGraw-Hill Book Co., 1960), p. 435.

do leave home go to various places. They sometimes go from one part of the city to another part, from one city to another, from a rural area to a city, or from one state to another.

Away from home the girls stay in various places. Some stay with friends and relatives. Others stay in hotels, apartments, rooming houses, maternity homes, foster homes, or wage homes. An unmarried mother should not go into lonely seclusion. Depending upon the circumstances, she should stay either with parents, friends, or relatives, or in a reputable maternity home or foster home.

The attitude of the woman toward the man responsible for the pregnancy varies according to the relationship between the two, the personality of the woman, and the responsibility assumed by the man in regard to the pregnancy. Some women show unconcern in regard to the man, others display abiding affection for the father of the child, and others express bitter hate for him.

Less is known about the unwed father than about the unwed mother, but he apparently can no more be categorized than can the unwed mother. The relationships which exist between unwed mothers and fathers vary from a long-term intimacy to a chance meeting. Frequently the girl is made pregnant by the only man with whom she has been sexually intimate. The responsibility assumed by the man also varies. Some offer to marry the woman and others provide financial support. However, many are elusive and avoid responsibility; frequently the man blames the girl for what has happened. By taking legal steps, the girl can usually force the man to assume financial responsibility. However, support injunctions are seldom strictly enforced, and it is difficult for the girl to obtain satisfactory support unless the man is willing to provide it.

The unwed mother follows various courses of action in regard to her baby. She either murders the baby, keeps the child with her, places it in a foster home, boarding home, or orphanage, or surrenders it for adoption. The majority of unwed mothers in maternity homes surrender their babies for adoption. Whether the mother keeps or surrenders the child must be her own decision. Which is best depends largely upon the individual. Generally speaking, however, adoption is best for both the mother and the child.

Three avenues are open to the girl who desires to surrender her baby for adoption: an approved adoption agency, the gray market, or the black market. The so-called black market is the practice by unscrupulous persons of selling babies for profit to couples who cannot qualify for children under agency restrictions. The black market is an abominable practice and should not be patronized. The so-called gray market is the practice by individuals, such as doctors and ministers, of placing babies in the homes of couples who desire a child but who do not wish to go through agency channels. Usually the man and wife who adopt the child pay the expenses of the unwed mother; other than this there are no fees. Although those who operate in the gray market usually have the noblest of motives, the results of such practices are often tragic. Because these individuals usually lack training in the complicated field of child placement, they often make poor placements. By far the best method of surrender is through a licensed adoption agency. These agencies employ trained personnel who work expertly for the best interest of the unwed mother, the child, and the adopting parents.

What happens afterward to those who have experienced pregnancy out of wedlock is not an easy question to answer. The very nature of the problem makes information almost inaccessible. However, on the basis of studies [4] which have been made, a few general statements can be set forth. Most of the women adjust and have reasonably normal lives. Many marry and have happy homes. If the man married is not the father of the child, the woman usually tells him about her out-of-wedlock pregnancy. Often a woman who keeps her child and does not marry proves to be a responsible mother. On the other hand, some women do not adjust and continue to lead tragic lives. A hasty marriage to the child's father often results in a loveless marriage or a broken home. Sometimes an unmarried mother who keeps her child is irresponsible and she ruins the child's life. A few unwed mothers bear other children out of wedlock.

Helping the Unwed Mother

Help for the unwed mother is not abundant, and what there is is not very accessible. Several reasons can be given for this lack of help. For example, some people feel that the unwed mother deserves to suffer for her sin and that to help her is to encourage her to have another out-of-wedlock pregnancy; actually, according to statistical studies and case records, the opposite is true. Also, many people are

---

[4] Dorothy Long, "A Follow-up Study of Unmarried Mothers," *Social Casework*, XXXVI (January, 1955), 27–33.

not aware of the problem of unwed mothers and are, therefore, in no position to offer help. As people have become aware of the large number of unwed mothers and of their difficult problems, many have become concerned and have worked to eliminate the cruel treatment practiced in former years.

The unwed mother needs help in a number of ways. She needs spiritual help—help in realizing and confessing her sin, help in developing faith in God and in herself, help in developing sound moral principles. She often needs physical help, such as food, shelter, early and lasting medical care, and financial assistance during and following her pregnancy. She needs help socially, especially when she re-enters the stream of community life. In almost every case she needs expert psychological help. Skilled guidance is needed to help her solve her emotional problems and to help her decide what she will do with her child.

Individuals will frequently be called on to help the unwed mother. Most girls turn first to individuals, not agencies; one survey revealed that less than 10 per cent had any dealing with a social agency. It is important, therefore, that the unwed mother go to the right individuals, and that these persons know how best to help. The persons most frequently consulted are ministers, professional persons—social workers, doctors, lawyers, teachers—and persons closely related to the unwed mother, such as parents, relatives, and friends.

The minister is often the first person to whom the unwed mother goes for help. During all contacts with the girl, his attitude should be that of helpfulness. At the initial interview he is neither to condemn nor condone her act; he is to follow the example of Jesus as he dealt with the woman taken in adultery. Later, when the girl has come to realize that his chief desire is to help her, the minister should lead the girl to understand the seriousness of her sin, encourage her to confess her sin, and help her to understand the nature of God's forgiveness. He will find the following Scriptures helpful in this regard: 1 Timothy 1:15; Hebrews 7:25; 1 John 1:9.

In most cases the minister should assist the girl in contacting the proper agency and then work with that agency insofar as possible. It is necessary, therefore, that he be familiar with the available agencies, so he can warn against unscrupulous agencies, nonprofessional help, and the black-market representatives. However, he should realize his own limitations and not assume the role of a trained social worker.

The following suggestions are made to individuals who seek to help unwed mothers: Do not appear shocked and horrified when the girl reveals her problem. Be reassuring; help her to realize that her whole life is not ruined. Do not try for easy solutions that relieve only temporary anxieties or solve temporary problems. Know the community resources well enough to be able to refer the person to the proper place for help. Keep printed material on hand that will be helpful to the unwed mother (such material can be obtained from the agencies listed at the end of this chapter). Try not to become too deeply involved; leave this to close relatives or better still to trained social workers. Work with the person as an individual, not as an "unmarried mother."

Agencies and institutions can also help the unwed mother. Among these helpful institutions stands the church. The church that is related to the girl should manifest a spirit of kindness and helpfulness, show a sympathetic understanding toward the parents, render financial assistance if it is needed, and pray for the girl and her family. Through the denomination, the churches should provide chaplains to give spiritual help to girls who are in maternity homes. If adequate maternity homes are not established by the state or by other groups, denominations might well have a valid ministry in providing such homes.

Each year maternity homes provide institutional care for approximately one fifth of the total number of known unwed mothers. The homes, numbering approximately two hundred, are sponsored by various groups and by individuals. The Florence Crittenton Homes Association and the Salvation Army operate the largest number of homes. Religious denominations, local groups, and individuals also support a number of homes.

The policies of the homes vary in regard to admission and fees. A few have racial restrictions on admission and some specify that only girls having their first out-of-wedlock child may enter. Generally speaking, however, about the only restrictions enforced in all the homes pertain to health and co-operation. Girls who have contagious diseases are not allowed to enter until they have been cured. Girls who are not willing to co-operate and comply with the regulations of the home are not accepted.

The fees vary according to the locality of the home, the sponsorship of the home, and the girl's ability to pay. Frequently, free service is available for girls who cannot pay. State or county departments of public welfare sometimes pay for the girl's care. In almost all cases the fees are nominal.

The concept of operation in most maternity homes is redemptive. The atmosphere is generally pleasant and cheerful. Recreational, educational, and religious activities are usually provided. Trained social workers are available to help the girls prepare for a well-adjusted life when they return to the mainstream of society.

There also is the foster home plan. A few agencies use only this one type of maternity care. Some girls require the more homelike facilities of the foster home.[5] The selection of the foster home is, of course, of great importance. Stable Christian families can render valuable service by volunteering to provide a foster home for unwed mothers.

Hospitals can also render service to the unwed mother. They should train personnel to safeguard the interests of the mother and child. The staff should be alert to signs which indicate that a woman coming in for the delivery of a child is pregnant out of wedlock. A specially trained caseworker should be available for such an occasion. Hospitals should establish policies to protect the mother and child—policies for guarding against illegal or ill-advised adoption practices, for preventing unidentified persons from taking the baby after discharge and for assuring secrecy.

Public service for the unwed mother is also available. Each state has a Department of Public Welfare which can provide helpful information and valuable assistance. Also many counties and cities have child welfare workers who can frequently render great aid and provide personal attention.

Preventing the Problem

A concerted effort should be made to prevent pregnancy out of wedlock. The basic strategy in attacking the problem is to eliminate immoral sexual activity. The pregnancy is a consequence or a symptom; the real problem is out-of-bounds sexual activity and the factors which encourage such activity. Since 70 per cent of the unwed mothers are under twenty-five, the bulk of preventive measures should be directed toward young people.

---

[5] For an excellent discussion of the advantages of the foster home plan, see Babette Block, "Foster Family Care for Unmarried Mothers" (Washington: U. S. Department of Health, Education, and Welfare, Children's Bureau, 1953).

Because the problem is complex, preventive measures must involve a number of factors. The religious aspect of prevention is extremely important. A program of adequate evangelism, coupled with a program of training in Christian living, is a basic necessity. The biblical concept of purity, chastity, and marital fidelity must be communicated to young people. It should be emphasized that while the sexual drive is basically good and has been given to man by God, the sexual act is to be exercised only within marriage (cf. Gen. 1:27; Ex. 20:14; 1 Cor. 7:39, Eph. 5:31). A proper code of sexual conduct and strong religious ideals should be cultivated among young people and adults. Constant effort must be made to motivate church members to commit themselves to dedicated Christian living.

Prevention also has a social aspect. Pregnancy out of wedlock is not an isolated phenomenon of immorality in society. The increase in the number of unwed mothers in the United States fits into a general pattern of moral decline. To attack the causes of the general moral sickness is to attack many of the causes of this particular problem. However, there are some steps which should be taken that will have a specific preventive force. Those social influences which encourage out-of-wedlock sexual relations should be eliminated as far as is possible. Young people should be warned about the influences which lead to premarital sexual relations. The social reasons for not indulging in such relations should be positively presented: (1) There is a definite possibility that pregnancy will result and bring with it catastrophic consequences; (2) guilt feelings usually arise and serious emotional disorders may result; (3) the possibility for real love, which is based not on gratification but on protection and unselfishness, is lessened; (4) the chances for a happy marriage are decidedly diminished.

Closely related to the religious and social aspects is the psychological-emotional aspect of prevention. The establishment of stable homes with proper parent-child relationships will go a long way toward eliminating serious psychological and emotional problems which lead to pregnancy out of wedlock. An adequate school counseling program will help young people overcome some of their serious emotional problems. Certain key persons in the community should be trained to recognize psychological danger signs and either counsel with those needing help or refer them to a more adequately trained person.

All aspects of prevention—religious, social, and psychological-emotional—are vital. Specific steps toward a solution to the problem of pregnancy out of wedlock should involve all three, but generally speaking, the key to prevention rests with the church, the community, and the family.

The minister in a church plays an important part in the campaign against extramarital sexual relations. He should minister to parents and children as families in order to strengthen the homes. He should preach on the place of sex in the Christian's life. He should counsel in group discussions and in private conferences to cultivate ideals, attitudes, and convictions which act as religious preventives. He should let it be known that he is available for individual counseling.

The church as a whole also plays a vital part in the prevention of pregnancy out of wedlock. The role that an individual church plays in the over-all effort for prevention will depend largely upon the size, location, and social theory of the church. Some activities, however, can be entered into by almost all churches. For example, churches should provide sex education which deals with the spiritual, biblical, and emotional aspects of sex as well as with the physical. Churches should also make their programs interesting and challenging to young people, distribute helpful literature, and strive to eliminate community influences which contribute to immorality.

Some churches are able to sponsor special programs which contribute to the prevention of pregnancy out of wedlock. For example, some churches sponsor special conferences for parents or conferences on family life. Some provide a large-scale recreational program; some have established a program of premarital and parental counseling. Probably the two greatest contributions which churches can make to the prevention of pregnancy out of wedlock are to lead young people to commit their lives to dedicated Christian living and to minister to homes to cultivate Christian family life.

Community government also has a key role to play in prevention. However, in the available materials on the subject, very little has been said about specific community actions. Some harsh but inadequate measures have been suggested. For example, it has been suggested that state aid be denied to unwed mothers who have more than two children, that unwed mothers who have more than two children be sterilized, and that the men involved in pregnancy out of wedlock be forced to provide financial support for the mother and child.

Basically, the positive task of the community, its leaders, and its government is to promote a wholesome community atmosphere. This task involves the elimination of social practices and influences which contribute to pregnancy out of wedlock. The task also involves careful city planning to prevent slums from developing and to provide adequate wholesome recreational activities.

Almost all authorities who work with unwed mothers agree that the home is the basic key to prevention. The proper care and training of children in the home is the best way to prevent pregnancy out of wedlock. Many excellent books have been written on family life and on parent-child relations; parents can receive much help from these books as they work to establish a healthy home environment.

Parental responsibility is heavy. Parents must provide discipline; they must be careful not to be either too strict or too lax. Children must be trained in decision-making so that they will not be easily swayed by the pressure of peers to indulge in activities which they know to be wrong. Parents should provide adequate sex education. Love should prevail in the home so that the child will not be forced to seek love and affection outside the home. Case studies indicate that a happy home atmosphere in which young people receive ample love and affection is the best insurance against pregnancy out of wedlock. Finally, parents should bring Christian influences to bear within the home and should teach their children the principles of Christian living.

Conclusion

The Christian has a twofold task in relation to the problem: (1) to help those who are already pregnant out of wedlock, and (2) to work toward prevention of others becoming so. In order to carry out his task, the Christian must understand the extent, effect, and cause of the problem.

If the Christian is to provide adequate help, he must be aware of the needs of unmarried mothers and of the means available to meet those needs. The unwed mother should be dealt with like any other person in need of help, like any other who has sinned and stands in need of God's forgiveness and of man's assistance.

Although it is not practical for all Christians to devote all of their time to working for the prevention of pregnancy out of wedlock, some should take the lead in a concentrated effort on the part of the church, the community, and the home. Religious, social, and psychological factors must be utilized to eliminate the causes. If the effort is to be effective, a simple moralistic approach must be abandoned and an intelligent approach which demonstrates an understanding of the complexity of the problem must be assumed.

The problem of pregnancy out of wedlock has too long received only casual attention from Christians. It demands careful attention. The two hundred thousand out-of-wedlock births recorded each year in the United States represent over half a million mothers, fathers, and children in desperate need of the help which Christians can provide. It is high time that Christians cease delivering pious words of censure and begin to demonstrate practical works of compassion for these moral outcasts of society.

Additional Reading

BUTCHER, RUTH L., and ROBINSON, MARION O. *The Unmarried Mother*. New York: Public Affairs Committee, 1959.

EDLIN, SARA B. *The Unmarried Mother in Our Society*. New York: Farrar, Straus & Cudahay, 1954.

Helping the Unmarried Mother and Her Child. Austin, Texas: The Texas Department of Public Welfare, 1953.

MORLOCK, MAUD, and CAMPBELL, HILARY. *Maternity Homes for Unmarried Mothers*. Washington: United States Department of Labor, Children's Bureau, 1946.

YOUNG, LEONTINE. *Out of Wedlock*. New York: McGraw-Hill Book Co., 1954.

Sources of Additional Information

Child Welfare League of America, Inc., 345 East 46th Street, New York, New York.

Family Service of America, 95 Madison Avenue, New York 16, New York.

Florence Crittenton Home Association, 608 South Dearborn Street, Chicago 5, Illinois.

National Association on Service to Unmarried Parents, 1881 Torbenson Drive, Cleveland 12, Ohio.

National Headquarters, The Salvation Army, 120 West 14th Street, New York, New York.

Sellers Baptist Home and Adoption Center, 2010 Peniston Street, New Orleans 15, Louisiana.

U. S. Department of Health, Education, and Welfare, Social Security Administration, Children's Bureau, Washington, D. C.

Women's Social Service Secretary, 34 Ellis Street, Atlanta 3, Georgia.

3

Homosexuality: A Christian Appraisal

G. RAY WORLEY

Irate parents approach their pastor. Their son informs them that he has been having sexual relations with a male youth leader in the church. They desire to prosecute the youth leader; the pastor seeks to avoid unfavorable publicity. The youth leader is confronted with the charge, confesses, is admonished, and is relieved of his position of leadership.

A young wife seeks her pastor's counsel. Her husband is seldom at home. At first she suspected another woman. Now she knows that he "pals around" with another man. She has been told that this is not a normal relationship. Her husband more and more avoids her. There are three children in the family. What should she do?

Two young women in a state school are constant companions. They become roommates and are seldom seen away from each other. Although one is fairly attractive, she refuses dates with boys who ask her. Her companion is less attractive, is aggressive, has a boyish bob, usually dresses in tailored suits, and is a little overbearing in personality. Whenever the younger and more feminine girl even speaks to another girl, it precipitates an embarrassing scene. The experienced dorm counselor strongly suspects latent or even overt homosexuality.

The increasing frequency of homosexual behavior poses a perplexing question to the conscientious minister. What can and should the church do when this problem arises? What is being done? Where can an individual turn for help? What is the possibility of helping such persons? What aggravates or causes homosexuality?

31

The intent of this study is to bring the problem of homosexuality into clear focus for leaders in a church situation. First, the problem will be discussed frankly in a factual manner. Second, the role of the church will be considered, endeavoring to set forth some suggestions for the minister and other church leaders. Third, some suggestions are made for parents who are confronted by this problem. Fourth, young people who become involved in such a relationship are given some guides for living which may enable them to overcome this plaguing problem. Remedial and preventive measures are recommended in the light of the total problem.

The Problem

Those concerned with the moral life of America were shocked when Kinsey reported that at least 37 per cent of the adult male population had some overt homosexual experience between adolescence and old age. Examination of the study indicates, however, that the group which was surveyed was not a true cross section of the American male population. Kinsey also included incidental experiences in his tabulation, rather than distinguishing the "true homosexual" from the occasional offender.

Regardless of criticism, Kinsey's study did awaken "ivory-tower thinkers" to a condition which had been oblivious to the casual observer. Rather than quibbling over the matter of degree, serious students were shocked into study and thought.

Definition.—Homosexuality has been defined as the preference by an individual for a person of the same sex, rather than a person of the opposite sex, as a sexual companion. "The homosexual is an individual endowed with sexual desires directed wholly or in part toward members of the same sex, and possessing characteristic psychic and physical traits of the opposite sex." [1] But in vernacular terms, "homosexuality is a state of being in love with one of the same sex," with this love finding a sexual outlet in the relationship. Rosanoff defines homosexuality as "a sexual peculiarity, occurring in more or less marked degree, characterized by a sexual attraction toward persons of the same, instead of the opposite, sex." [2]

---

[1] Benjamin Karpman, *The Sexual Offender and His Offenses* (New York: The Julian Press, 1954), p. 13.

[2] Aaron J. Rosanoff, *Manual of Psychiatry and Mental Hygiene* (New York: John Wiley & Sons, 1949), p. 1053.

The homosexual may actually have physical relations with a person of the same sex. This is called *overt* homosexuality. A person may be simply attracted to a person of the same sex, to the exclusion of attractions toward persons of the opposite sex, perhaps accompanied by dreams, fantasy, and erotic behavior. Such a person may be termed a *latent* homosexual. The likeness is in the orientation of affection and desire toward a person of the same sex; the difference has to do with an overt sexual act with a person of the same sex.

There are two distinct roles in the homosexual relation. Usually, an individual functions predominantly in one role. A homosexual may be either an aggressor, initiating the act and fulfilling the pseudo-male function of penetration in pederasty, or a passive participant. There is no hard and fast distinction, because various methods and relationships are established between homosexuals.

The act of homosexuality usually falls under one of four categories: (1) fellatio, or oral-genital contact; (2) cunnilingus, or oral-vaginal contact; (3) buggery, or genital-anal contact; (4) mutual masturbation. Sodomy is a term used to designate all "crimes against nature"—carnal copulation in any of certain unnatural ways.

The passive partner is usually the one who is penetrated in buggery, or who performs the act of fellatio or masturbation in instances where it is not mutual. The aggressor, however, may be largely responsible for initiating the relationship, and even coerce the passive member into the relationship. This is especially true of young boys who are induced or coerced into the first relationship, not infrequently through a money bribe or by a threat of force.

Not infrequently a person may engage in both heterosexual and homosexual relations. Some may be considered in a bisexual category. However, Bergler believes that the person who is homosexual for any length of time has a predisposition to that function and is not a bisexual.[3]

The frequency and circumstances surrounding sexual behavior determine to a large degree the individual's sexual nature. A person in a sexually segregated institution or group may not be a confirmed homosexual just because he engages in homosexual relations. Not infrequently such an individual will revert to a heterosexual role to the exclusion of any homosexual contact when thrown with the opposite

[3] Edmund Bergler, *Homosexuality: Disease or Way of Life* (New York: Hill & Wang, 1956), p. 108.

sex. Should this individual again be placed in a sexually segregated setting, he may again become homosexual.

Bergler's contention that there is no true bisexual seems sound. Individuals may function bisexually, but this does not indicate that they are firmly entrenched in the heterosexual role, or they would not seek the homosexual relation. Moreover, the theory that "saving of face" is involved in the heterosexual role seems sound. Bergler contends that "the supposed bisexual is a homosexual with some mechanical potency retained—until further notice." However, his distinction is more applicable to a person who is a confirmed homosexual rather than an offender who is predisposed because the environment fails to provide normal sexual release through heterosexual relations.[4]

Causes.—What causes homosexuality? Various theories have been proposed. Genetic disorder has been suggested, but studies are inconclusive. Hooker cites studies which lend negative results, but says, "Nevertheless, the assumption that complicated genetic factors may, in *some* cases, *indirectly* exert an influence, must remain open to question, in view of possible future refinements of research methods at present too gross to prove or disprove the theory." [5]

Research thus far does not indicate any basis for claiming that homosexuality is constitutional. Berg and Allen say, "We can state with confidence that there is no discernible difference between the physique of the homosexual and heterosexual by any tests, microscopical, macroscopical, biochemical, or endocrine, of which we are aware at present." [6] Hooker believes that the expanding field of biochemistry may throw more light on this matter.

Hooker too readily dismisses the psychoanalytic school of thought. Perhaps this is occasioned by the diversity of opinion prevailing among psychiatrists. She notes the failure of the homosexual to identify with the parent of the same sex and an overidentification or

---

[4] It can be pointed out, however, that an individual may become addicted to homosexual relations while in sexually segregated conditions. This may carry over into relations in normally constituted society. Edmund Bergler, *One Thousand Homosexuals* (Paterson, N. J.: Pageant Books, Inc., 1959), p. 107.

[5] Evelyn Hooker, "Homosexuality—Summary of Studies," *Sex Ways—In Fact and Faith: Bases for Christian Family Policy,* eds. Evelyn M. and Sylvanus M. Duvall (New York: Association Press, 1961), p. 169.

[6] Charles Berg and Clifford Allen, *The Problem of Homosexuality* (New York: Citadel Press, 1958), p. 43.

excessive attachment to the parent of the opposite sex. Most commonly observed is the disturbance of relationships with the parents and an overattachment to the mother.

Homosexuality, it is posited, represents the arresting of a normal social development, with a corresponding fixation of sexual development and social relationship at a distinct level of personal, psychical, sexual satisfaction. Normally, children pass through three broad stages of development. The first stage is the erotic stage, wherein the child seeks its own personal satisfaction above all else. The desire for warmth, food, relief from personal irritation, and for personal security prevails. A second broad area of development is characterized by interest in one of the same sex. The child feels more at ease with those of his own sex. It is not abnormal to develop crushes for those of his own sex. By the time of puberty, however, the child is beginning to notice persons of the opposite sex. There is aroused not only an interest in but a desire to be noticed by and to be with one of the opposite sex. The normal result of this development is courtship, marriage, and the establishment of a home. Obviously, if development is arrested before the cycle is completed, the individual becomes fixated at that point. This, in part, explains the homosexual.

Bergler sets forth an additional thesis. He has noted a quality in persons which he terms psychic masochism. The masochist is one who receives pleasure from pain being inflicted on him. The psychic masochist seeks to be hurt. He is an "injustice collector." For this reason, the homosexual—who is a psychic masochist, plus—cannot sustain a continuing relationship with a partner. This is the reason for Bergler's refutation of the claim that homosexuality is as normal for some as heterosexuality is for others. Since the homosexual seeks to be punished, either through creating a situation which draws criticism from family or friends, or through creating scenes which result in unhappiness and more "injustice collecting," he is a psychic masochist and can never be permanently happy in a homosexual relationship.

Bergler places the roots of psychic masochism in the first eighteen months of a child's life. Rather than blaming parents, as is commonly done, he believes that the child selects those stimuli from his environment which he will receive as meaningful, and thus the individual is responsible.

Hooker is aware of the elusive nature of any adequate answer when she observes "that homosexuality is an extraordinarily complicated phenomenon, in which the causative factors are multiple." Contributing factors perhaps include:

Inappropriate identification with the opposite-sexed parent; fear of hostility to either parent; reversal of masculine and feminine roles in parents; cultural overemphasis on the stereotype of "masculinity," which produces feelings of inadequacy in males who are not able to fulfil this expectation; rigid dichotomy of male and female social roles, with failure to allow for individuals who do not fit easily into either of these; and easier access to sexual gratification with members of one's own sex in adolescence, resulting in habit patterns which persist.[7]

Because of the church's role as a teacher of sound family life, contributing to a wholesome understanding of self and sound values for family and personal living, it cannot ignore the problems which homosexuality indicates do exist. Rather than castigating the persons involved, the church should become concerned with the persons who are homosexuals. Instead of regarding them as moral outcasts, the church should consider their activity as a symptom of even deeper-seated problems.

Accompanying factors.—Along with consideration of the various theories concerning the origin of homosexuality, it is appropriate to survey the phenomena which accompany the development of homosexuals. Karpman notes factors which may have an effect upon the incidence of homosexuality.

Authorities are divided with regard to constitutional factors. Some believe that homosexuality is an inherited condition. Others believe that it is the result of the human personality's maladjustment to environment. Certain hereditary factors do determine the physical makeup of the individual. This may greatly affect the social adjustment of the youth whose life is gradually molded in response to his environment. But evidence that a biological factor predisposes to homosexuality is too hypothetical to be considered sound.

Various facets of the environment do contribute to the child's development; environmental conditions help to determine choices which the youth must make. "No single factor of background or personality determines a boy's general behavior for good or bad in later or early life; morbid personality factors, stemming from un-

---

[7] *Op. cit.,* pp. 171–72.

healthy background influences, determine juvenile general offenses which are in continuity with later general crimes." [8]

To the extent that socioeconomic matters affect an individual's adjustment to life, to that extent the homosexual may be influenced in the development of his deviate pattern. The relation of these factors to the normal expression of the sex urge is important. Sometimes a lack of money may cause a boy to be enticed by the lure of pay for privileges.

An emotional disorder stemming from childhood is prevalent in most cases. Frequently, there is neglect, rejection, domination, brutality, overindulgence, confusion of the sexual role, poor example, immaturity in parent passed on to the child, lack of proper training in self-control, lack of proper supervision, or any of the multitudinous problems evidenced in and causal of broken homes. These contribute to the development of a homosexual. Perhaps the most significant sign is an overidentification with the mother.

Seduction, precocious stimulation, and castration threats produce an emotional trauma in a child. Seduction by adults is extremely dangerous to the youth. "The need for children to re-experience sexual gratification with adults is often inordinate once the pattern has been established." [9] However, either the child must have psychological factors which make him susceptible to this seduction, or else the habit must become firmly engrained in the individual's experience.

In alcoholism, the homosexual may attempt to sublimate the latent tendencies, only to find that intoxication breaks the power of sublimation and permits indulgence which would never have occurred in the sober state. The indication is that latent homosexuality is exposed in the alcoholic state. The alcoholic homosexual is more apt to resort to violence than would be true of other homosexuals.

In all cases constructive, positive factors are notably lacking in the life of the homosexual.

Symptoms.—What symptoms may be considered as indicative of homosexuality? Several suggestions may assist the minister, church leader, or parent who is confronted with the probability of homosexuality.

Catching a person engaging in an overt homosexual act or securing an open admission of participation in overt acts may indicate

---

[8] Karpman, *op. cit.,* p. 77.
[9] *Ibid.,* p. 86.

addiction to homosexuality. However, not every homosexual act signifies that a person is a homosexual.

When sexual dreams are built of fantasies based on relations with one of the same sex, this is a symptom of latent homosexuality.

Another symptom is the confusion of sexual roles by a child. Although playing may occasion dressing up as one of the opposite sex, a prolonged identification with one of the opposite sex is a danger signal.

Prolonged crushes in adolescence with one of the same sex may be a danger signal, indicating that the individual is only in the second stage of the normal three-cycle personality development.

Some psychiatrists have pointed to excessive embraces, particularly on the part of women in club meetings, as indicative of latent homosexuality.

The phenomenon of dress may be a sign of either latent or overt homosexuality. In overt male homosexuals, dress is more a sign of the role assumed in the homosexual relationship, with the passive homosexual tending to dress as a woman. Some pose as female impersonators, and dress accordingly. However, dress alone does not always indicate the fact of homosexuality or indicate the participant's role.

The existence of emotional disturbance in youth may indicate a personality condition which may later find its manifestation in homosexuality.

The Church's Role

Ordinarily, the church has largely ignored the homosexual when not engaged in condemning him. However, since the membership of the church has been infiltrated by this deviate practice, and since the minister is often confronted with the necessity of counseling homosexuals, a more serious consideration of the problem by the church is past due.

Responsibility.—What is the responsibility of the church to the homosexual? The church should be concerned for his spiritual and moral well-being, just as much as for any person outside the fellowship of the redeemed. The Bible does give some admonitions concerning the homosexual, but the major emphasis in the Bible is upon recognizing that the practicing homosexual is outside the kingdom of God (1 Cor. 6:9). Paul indicates in Romans 1:24, 26–27, that the homosexuals are those who have neglected and rejected God and continue in their chosen way of life.

The biblical writers always condemn sin; but at the same time, there is an abiding interest in the sinner. Homosexuality does not constitute the unforgivable sin, but it does indicate the perilous condition of the one who continues the practice.

The practicing homosexual alienates himself from the redeemed community in the church. God's laws are given to man in community. By rejecting God's law for man in community, the homosexual must also reject God. At least, the homosexual is less than God has intended man to be. Because of the emphasis upon the satiation of physical desires, the homosexual becomes an addict, or becomes hypnotized by the sexual stimulus of the homosexual act. Putting emphasis on self-satisfaction, the homosexual cannot give God the central place in his life.

Knowing the spiritual, as well as some of the emotional factors involved, the church has a responsibility to be concerned for the life of the homosexual.

Limitations.—It is important for the leaders and ministers of the church to recognize the dire psychological imbalance of the homosexual. Practical experience will bear out the folly of giving "pat" and shallow answers to those who are involved in homosexuality. Above all, the church leader must realize that the prognosis for a homosexual is very poor, even in the hands of a skilled psychiatric practitioner. Without help it is almost folly for a pastor to seek to adequately counsel with a homosexual. The church leader has a proper function, but it is well for him to recognize his limitations in the field of counseling. A wholesome relation between the church leader, particularly the minister, and a psychiatrist or psychological counselor will enable the minister to refer a homosexual to the man specifically trained in the area of counseling. It will also permit the minister to be available for consultation in religious matters as concern and interest along this line may develop in the counseling process.

Bergler is emphatic in insisting that the homosexual must want to change before therapy will be of any benefit to him. It is important to determine the precise motivation behind the homosexual's seeking the counsel of a minister. If this counsel is just to appease a relative or spouse, or to temporarily ease a troubled conscience, then the prognosis may be very poor. If, however, the homosexual consults the minister out of a deep sense of guilt and as a genuine expression of concern for changing his life pattern, then the minister can feel justified in devoting time to this needy person.

Above all, the church leader and minister must recognize the wisdom of referral and accept the limited prognosis usually given to homosexual addicts.

Positive values.—Since homosexuality springs from an impoverished emotional background, or one that is distorted, the church has limitless resources to pour into this vacuum. The minister should seek to determine what contributed to the development of the homosexual. If environmental factors have contributed significantly, the church needs to honestly assess its ministry to individuals and families in order to help eliminate conditions contributing to homosexuality. The church can speak to the individual in terms of a meaningful future.

The church can assure the homosexual of God's love and concern. It can speak of God's desire and willingness to forgive sin and accept the sinner into fellowship with Christ Jesus. However, the necessity for repentance and complete committal must be declared. The church can promise a new sense of well-being. It can make provision for those personal emotional qualities which the homosexual evidently lacks and has been seeking through his deviate behavior. The redeeming power of the gospel can be brought to bear on the life of the homosexual, if there is a deep and genuine desire to come into a right relationship with God.

Practical problems.—If the church is located in a small village or suburban area, the occasion for ministering to homosexuals may be less, and the problems involved in such a counseling role may be greater. In a city the cloak of anonymity shelters the homosexual who may consult a minister and begin to attend his church.

If the minister is faced with a problem involving the seduction of a youth as a consequence of participation in the church program, prompt action needs to be taken. The homosexual must be restrained from doing further damage to others and to himself. He should be relieved of places of responsibility and leadership where he may spread his social and spiritual maladjustment.

A problem of criminal liability may be involved. The pastor and church leaders should realize this. If the parties involve an adult and a juvenile, most states provide for criminal prosecution. The Christian has an obligation to consider other matters as being more important than mere prosecution, although this may be the best process to follow. If a person is permitted to continue this deviate behavior, other children may be molested or permanently damaged by being coerced or seduced into homosexual activity.

Often community feeling is considered most important. Not infrequently, adverse community feeling would be created if the problem were given public attention. This might work ultimately to the detriment of the total church program. Particularly would this be true if the offender has been on the church staff. The situation is always bad enough without displaying it before the public through legal action with its attendant (and sometimes glaringly inaccurate) publicity.

Regardless of the circumstances, the offender should be relieved of leadership roles in the church and should be carefully supervised in all of his relationships within the church program.

When the occurrence of homosexuality involves the paid staff of a church, the lay leadership must recognize the seriousness of the problem. Unfortunately, the prognosis is very poor for helping a person to function effectively in the "fish-bowl" life of a church while under psychiatric care for deep-seated problems such as are involved in homosexuality. If the individual is only a latent homosexual—never participating in an overt act—then prognosis is more favorable, provided the offender is amenable to accepting counseling help.

Discretion is the great need. The cause of Christ faces enough obstacles without besmirching the name of a good church which has the misfortune of having a homosexual on its staff. The scriptural admonition (cf. Gal. 6:1, 10), which counsels Christian leaders to seek to restore an erring brother in a spirit of meekness, is not inappropriate. However, this concern and desire to handle a matter discreetly and in a Christian manner must not be considered a weakness.

Toleration is needed for the individual, but the work and ministry of the church cannot be unduly shackled by inept leadership. A practicing homosexual can hardly give the type of leadership needed in a Christian church. The emotional difficulties attendant upon homosexuality are too burdensome for the offender to be able to function capably in the demanding role of a vocational Christian worker. The homosexual has no place in the leadership of a church. However, the church may acknowledge its responsibility to minister to the homosexual, just as it would to any other needy person. But the church should not tolerate homosexuality among its leadership.

Counsel for Parents

Parents should proceed with care when they suspect that a youth is engaging in homosexual relations. Aberrant behavior should not be confused with homosexuality. A certain amount of "chumminess" and participation in "gang" relationships is normal and to be expected among youth of the same age. Experimentation and exploration on the part of children is to a degree perfectly normal. If, however, there is a fixation at any point in the development of normal social relations, so that the youth does not develop properly, but seeks the companionship of his own sex to the exclusion of relationships with the opposite sex, then there may be cause for alarm.

For parents who suspect latent homosexuality or whose children are ensnared by a practicing homosexual, several things may be recommended: (1) Consult with a trained counselor. This problem is too complex for the ordinary individual to handle without the help of an experienced and trained counselor. (2) Seek to analyze personal relationships within the home. Not infrequently, homosexuality, like most delinquent situations, may be a symptom of an underlying strain in the home situation. (3) Both parents should cultivate the interest and companionship of the youth. If the youth had found satisfactory personal acceptance and emotional nourishment in the home, it is doubtful that he would have looked outside the home for acceptance and sexual release through deviate behavior. Attention needs to be centered on good personal relationships. (4) Try to involve the youth in new activities, new friends, and new relationships. Sometimes a change of environment will assist a youth, who is only casually involved in a homosexual relationship, to throw off the tendency to find personal acceptance and emotional relief through the deviate activity.

Counsel for Youth

Youth should be informed concerning the practice and prevalence of homosexuality. One minister mentioned a noted case involving a murder which resulted in the execution of a homosexual. When his teen-age children expressed ignorance of the meaning of the term, he was able to explain it to them in a wholesome manner.

If a youth is approached by a homosexual, the following is advised: (1) Refuse to have anything to do with the individual. (2) Notify parents and responsible authorities, including teachers and administrative leaders. In a church or civic group, the person who supervises the offending person should be notified. A policeman, the sheriff, or the district attorney will lend assistance. (3) Warn the one who makes the approach that you are not interested and will not hesitate to expose him.

If a youth becomes ensnarled in a homosexual relationship, and wants to break it, the following suggestions may prove helpful: (1) Consult a trained counselor. Perhaps your minister may be able to help or at least recommend a trained counselor to you. (2) Discuss the matter thoroughly with both parents, if possible. (3) Make a clean break—no tapering off. (4) Undertake a strenuous program involving some form of physical activity. (5) Avoid circumstances involving a possible compromising situation. (6) Seek to cultivate normal relationships with both those of the same sex and the opposite sex. Major on healthy group activities. (7) If the situation warrants, and the pastor or other counselor so advise, go to the police or other legal authorities. (8) Do not threaten the other person involved in the relationship. His fear of apprehension or his sense of guilt may lead to violence. (9) Remember that the police or other legal authorities will provide protection from retaliation by a spurned friend. "Hell hath no fury like a woman spurned" applies as appropriately to the offended party in a homosexual relationship when a break is made, and the homosexual is apt to have a personality disorder which is more volatile than a mere jealous person. (10) Recognize that any damage done is not irreparable. There is hope both of forgiveness by God and of a reclaimed, meaningful life.

Conclusion

Homosexuality is a psychological, sociological, and sexual phenomenon with spiritual implications. A person cannot be a homosexual and be rightly related to the society which God has prescribed for his children. In reality, homosexuality should be considered as a symptom of a deep psychological and spiritual need. Much care is needed in working with homosexuals, because their major problems are psychological in origin. The homosexual can be cured, provided there is a deep and genuine desire to change.

The homosexual is more to be pitied than scorned. To the evangelical Christian, the homosexual may be an enigma, a scapegoat, or a challenge; he provides a test for Christian love and understanding. In order to effect salvation, a pervasive reorientation of life is required, without compromise or partial reform. Many hours of conferences may be needed. Deepened understanding must be achieved, negating a cheap gospel of forgiveness that does little more than temporarily salve guilt feelings.

Work with homosexuals is definitely a specialized ministry. It requires adequate preparation and training in counseling. The responsibility for needy persons should not be shirked but should call the concerned Christian to more committed effort. Serving him who was the friend of "publicans and sinners," the Christian must seek for bridges of understanding and modes of communication which may enable an aberrant sexual deviate to become a maturing citizen in God's kingdom.

Additional Reading

BAILEY, DERRICK SHERWIN. *Sexual Relation in Christian Thought.* New York: Harper & Bros. 1959.

COLE, WILLIAM GRAHAM. *Sex in Christianity and Psychoanalysis.* New York: Oxford University Press, 1955.

KARPMAN, BENJAMIN. *The Sexual Offender and His Offenses.* New York: The Julian Press, 1954.

PIPER, OTTO. *The Biblical View of Sex and Marriage.* New York: Charles Scribner's Sons, 1960.

PLOSCOWE, MORRIS. *Sex and the Law.* New York: Prentice-Hall, 1951.

4

Birth Control—
Right or Wrong?

JAMES M. ROBINSON

The controversy over the morality of birth control has raged for hundreds of years, and yet it is a controversy which is as modern as today. In fact, it seems that never before has the question, "Is birth control right or wrong?" demanded an answer from the Christian minister as it does today.

There are many reasons why the current demand for an answer is so great. One of these reasons is the widespread use of some form of birth control among married couples of today. A medical doctor has declared his belief that 100 per cent of intelligent, normally fertile couples practice it for a time during their married life. Certainly, an ethical problem of this size and proportion cannot be overlooked by the minister who is genuinely concerned about helping his people find the right solution to moral issues.

A great many people are not only involved when birth control is in question but they are also genuinely confused about the morality of the practice. Although they know how, and do, practice birth control, at least occasionally, they are still not certain that what they are doing is completely right in the sight of God. So many ministers have ignored this controversial issue and so many denominational groups have neglected to take a stand on it that the modern Christian finds himself practically void of guidance in this area. It is time for Christian ministers to form some personal convictions concerning the morality of birth control from which they can speak to the need of the people.

Causes of the Present Controversy

Several causes have come together to make birth control the moral issue that it is today. Whether or not man has the right to seek to control the birth of children into his family has been subject to debate for centuries, but only within the last hundred years or so has the issue begun to take on the size and importance with which it is now characterized. Causes of the present controversy are both social and religious in nature.

Birth control as such was not a real issue either socially or morally until an English clergyman, Thomas Malthus, published in 1798, "Essay on the Principles of Population." In his essay, Malthus warned of the danger of overpopulation of the world and advised as a corrective either celibacy or late marriage. He made no mention of any mechanical method of birth control and probably would have frowned upon such a practice. Others quickly joined Malthus in his warning against overpopulation. Soon, however, some began to go beyond what Malthus had set forth as a possible way of averting the danger. England became a hotbed of controversy as Jeremy Bentham and Francis Place began to campaign among the masses for a specific mechanical method of birth control.

That the controversy should span the Atlantic was inevitable. The first American tract on birth control was "Moral Physiology," published by Robert Dale Owen in 1830. This work was followed in 1832 by Dr. Charles Knowlton's influential book, *Fruits of Philosophy*. This book resulted in a three-month jail sentence for the author and became the subject of a famous trial in England which, of course, greatly expedited its sale. In America the birth control movement was finally legitimatized by means of the work done by Margaret Higgins Sanger. Mrs. Sanger was a trained nurse and social worker in New York City, where she became appalled at the number of women suffering from the ill effects of too frequent and unwanted pregnancies. She dedicated her life to the rescue of these unfortunate women. Though she was persecuted, jailed, and constantly beset by difficulties, she finally succeeded in gaining the recognition and approval of the majority concerning the work she was doing.

The work done by Malthus and particularly by those who followed him was done on the social level. Birth control was set forth as the solution to a social problem, and the publicity led to its adoption by many and brought the issue concerning its morality out into the open. In this way Thomas Malthus and the neo-Malthusians contributed to the rise of the present controversy.

The present controversy has arisen also because of changing social conditions. Social conditions today seem to make some method of controlling the number of children born to a particular family a necessity. In modern times a new economy has come into being. Urban life has largely replaced rural life. Children who were once economic assets, in that they were able to contribute their labor in farm production, have now become liabilities, since they are able to contribute little or nothing to the financial stability of an urban family. The cost of living continues to rise so that the average couple today cannot afford to care for as many children as it would be physically possible for them to produce, nor are the houses of today built for occupancy by large families. These economic factors make the morality of birth control a vital issue.

Further social change is evidenced by the new high in living standards. Today's children are expected to be born in a hospital and the expectant mother to be under the constant care of a competent family doctor, if not a specialist. Children are to be given the opportunity of a higher education and generally must live on a higher level than the children of the past. Obviously, this means that the family must contain fewer children than would have been possible under previous standards of living. But is it right for a couple to attempt to limit the size of their family?

Changing social conditions have brought into sharp focus the importance of birth control.

One of the causes of the present controversy over the morality of birth control is religious in nature. This evinces the continuing influence of the early ascetics. In the days immediately following the apostolic period there developed a view that the desire for children was the only justification for sexual union. Clement of Alexandria summed up the attitude that came into vogue, as he said, "Intercourse performed licitly is an occasion of sin, unless done purely to beget children." [1]

Sexual union for any purpose was regarded as a mark of imperfection, and celibacy and continence within marriage were elevated as the

---

[1] Simon P. Wood (trans.), "The Fathers of the Church," *Clement of Alexandria* (New York: Fathers of the Church, 1954), XXXIII, 175.

goal to be sought by all. Sex was held to be a thing of this world, and the Christian was to separate himself from the world in preparation for the world which would soon come. Traces of this attitude still linger in the present day. There are still those who really see sex as something to be shunned and, if engaged in at all, to be engaged in purely for the purpose of procreation. It is not difficult to see that those holding this view would quickly engage in open controversy with those advocating the use of some method of birth control to allow participation in sexual union without conception.

The Heart of the Controversy

If the modern minister is to find for himself a position in regard to the practice of birth control, and if he is to help his people to do so, he must first determine what actually constitutes the heart of the controversy. He must get to the center of the matter rather than spending his time in the fringe areas. When he does this, he will find that the moral issue involved in the use of birth control is something other than that which it is often held to be.

The controversy today usually centers around the method used rather than around man's right to exercise birth control. Thus, determining legitimate means of preventing conception has become the problem. The position of the Roman Catholic Church is largely responsible for the centering of the controversy at this point.[2]

The Catholic Church holds that the primary purpose of marriage is procreative. Any positive, deliberate attempt to prevent conception and thus procreation is considered sinful. However, the Catholic Church holds that there are methods of birth control which do not involve positive and deliberate attempts to prevent conception, and these are distinguished from methods which it calls "artificial." It approves the "natural" methods and condemns the "artificial" or mechanical. The natural methods are continence and indulgence in intercourse only during the time when conception is physically impossible because of the lack of the presence of the female egg. The latter method is usually called the use of the "safe period."

The Catholic Church defends its position of the condemnation of the mechanical methods of birth control chiefly by an appeal to

---

[2] For a full discussion of the Roman Catholic position on birth control see John L. Thomas, *Marriage and Rhythm* (Westminster, Md.: The Newman Press, 1957).

natural law. The use of anything mechanical is said to introduce an unnatural element into the act of intercourse and thus to be contrary to the will of God. However, the objective observer is quick to realize that nature cannot be safely relied upon to act as a guide in moral matters. The natural course of disease is death, but God has given man dominion over nature so that he is free to labor to halt this natural consequence. The natural thing is for a man's beard to grow, and the razor is purely a mechanical device, but no one would hold the man who shaves to be immoral for that reason. Thus, so-called natural law ceases to be a reason for the condemnation of mechanical birth control methods.

The Catholic Church also appeals to other arguments in its condemnation of artificial birth control. It has said that the use of artificial birth control methods will allow lust to control marriage, will corrupt public morality, will cause damage to health, will produce ill-fitted children, will destroy the economic balance of the country, and will lead to race suicide. Yet, most of these arguments would apply as well to any method of birth control, and none of them need be true.

The position of the Roman Catholic Church is illogical. The Church frowns upon a deliberate attempt to prevent conception and yet, obviously, the indulgence in intercourse only during the "safe period" is exactly that. If God's primary purpose for the establishment of marriage were procreative, then the use of the "safe period" method would become just as much a frustration of his divine purpose as the use of any other method would be. When viewed from this standpoint, the question to be answered in determining the morality of birth control is seen to be not what method can be rightly used but whether any method is permissible in the sight of God.

The thing that must first be determined by the minister as he attempts to decide upon the morality of birth control is whether family limitation is ever permitted by God to the individual couple. Certainly, God intends for marriage to produce children, but when the question is asked as to whether God would ever permit a couple to take steps to limit the size of their family, certain practical considerations indicate a positive answer. One of these considerations is the health of the mother. Too frequent pregnancies can destroy maternal health. Also, pregnancy under certain physical conditions can jeopardize the life of the mother. Surely, God would permit the limitation of birth in a case where a pregnancy or additional pregnancies would endanger the health or life of the mother.

An additional practical consideration is the health and welfare of the child being pondered. Surely, God would not demand parenthood from the husband and wife, either of whom has a defect or disease which would certainly or even probably be passed on to the child. Too, statistics indicate that spaced children are healthier on the whole than those who are born as often as nature permits.

Not only does it seem that the health of the child ought to be safeguarded by every possible means, but also that consideration ought to be given to the probable ability of the parents to provide adequate care and education for the child. If the chances are that a child or additional children would be denied the right of health or proper care, it seems reasonable to assume that God, under these circumstances, would permit a couple to limit the number of children in their family.

Aside from these practical considerations, certain biblical principles are relevant and indicate a positive answer to the question. The worth of the individual and the value of life are taught (cf. Gen. 1:26, Ex. 20:13). These principles indicate that neither the life, health, nor welfare of the prospective child, nor that of the prospective mother, is to be considered unimportant in regard to the question of family limitation. The Bible also teaches the responsibility of the parents for the nurture and care of the child (cf. Eph. 6:4). This responsibility must be considered and accepted before the birth of a child is planned. Sexual union is to occupy a high and important place in marriage (cf. 1 Cor. 7:3, 5). This would seem to exclude the possibility of its being used only when the birth of a child is desired.

It is true that in Genesis 1:28, God told Adam and Eve to "be fruitful and multiply." At first glance this would seem to teach that God would be displeased with any attempt at family limitation. However, upon closer examination of this verse of Scripture it becomes evident that these words were spoken more as a blessing upon Adam and Eve than as a command to them. Nowhere does the Bible expressly forbid the limitation by man of his family, although the experience of Onan, recorded in Genesis 38:9–10, is sometimes used to teach the sinfulness of birth control. A study of the background of these verses reveals that the sin of Onan was not birth control but the breaking of the law of levirate marriage. Scriptural considerations, then, back up practical considerations in giving a positive answer to the question, "Will God ever permit family limitation?"

There is a second question that must be answered as the minister seeks to decide upon man's right to control birth. Is sexual union for purposes other than procreation permissible in the sight of God? If there is no other justifiable reason for sexual union, then birth control is clearly wrong. Once again, practical considerations seem to indicate that the question must be answered in the positive.

One of these practical considerations is the strength of the mating urge within man. It does not seem reasonable that God would have put such a strong sexual drive within man if that drive were to be exercised only during three or four brief periods in a lifetime. Would he not have instilled a drive that was intermittent and one that would have allowed response only during the time when conception or pregnancy would be possible?

The very fact that there are times when intercourse is possible though pregnancy is not indicates that God will allow sexual union for purposes other than procreation. During pregnancy further conception is impossible. At times other than during ovulation, pregnancy is impossible. In fact, the time when pregnancy is a possibility is but a minute fraction of the time when it is not. Would this be true if intercourse were to be indulged in only for the purpose of having children?

There are couples who discover in the early days of their marriage that they are sterile. Are they to remain continent through the rest of their married years because their sexual union cannot be for procreative purposes? These practical considerations make it difficult to believe that there are not other reasons justified in the sight of God for sexual union.

The Scriptures lend their weight to a positive answer to the question of whether sexual union for purposes other than procreation is permissible to man. The Bible indicates, in Genesis 2:18, that the purpose of marriage is not procreation but companionship. God created Adam and set him in the midst of a garden. Adam, however, was alone, and when God saw that this was not good, he determined to make an adequate helper for him who would be his companion and partner. The motive of procreation is not even mentioned. God's primary purpose in the institution of marriage was fellowship between husband and wife. This is not to say that the purpose of procreation does not enter the picture at all, for it does, but rather that there are other equally important purposes of marriage.

In both 1 Corinthians 6:16 and Matthew 19:5-6, the Bible emphasizes the unitive effects of sexual intercourse. It is by means of this intercourse that two people become one. This union of husband and wife into one flesh seems to be the primary purpose of the sexual relationship. It is impossible to find solid biblical support for the contention that procreation is the only legitimate purpose of sexual union.

If family limitation is ever permissible, as there is every reason to believe it must be under some circumstances, and if sexual union is justified for reasons other than the desire for children, then it is apparent that God does at times extend to man the right to prevent conception. The heart of the controversy over the morality of birth control rests here. What must be determined is when man has a right to control birth and when he does not. When is the practice of birth control right and when is it wrong?

Solution to the Controversy

The responsibility for the decision as to when birth control is right and when it is wrong rests with the individual couple. The Bible indicates that family limitation is sometimes permissible and that sexual union may be accomplished apart from procreative purposes, but it leaves the individual couple to decide for themselves whether or not God would permit family limitation or the use of birth control in their particular case. However, there are some considerations which will help the couple to know God's will for them.

In seeking to know if birth control is right or wrong for them, the couple must consider their responsibility before God to bear children. Marriage is God's plan for insuring the continued population of the world. Men and women have a responsibility for co-operation in this plan of God. But parenthood is much more than a responsibility. It is one of life's greatest blessings. The noted authority on marriage, David R. Mace, says that "nothing cements the unity of man and wife like the solemn wonder of that exalted moment when they stand together, hand in hand, looking down upon their sleeping child." [3] Only in extremely rare cases could a couple find justification for failing

---

[3] *Success in Marriage* (Nashville: Abingdon Press, 1958), pp. 130-31.

to fulfil their responsibility to God and for depriving themselves of the unique thrill of parenthood.

The minister who would give guidance to a couple concerning the use of birth control must remind them of their responsibility for bearing children and point out to them that the practice would be wrong without a valid reason for prevention or delay of pregnancy. Too, he must remind them that many reasons often given for the use of birth control are not valid. God would not be pleased with the couple who simply because of their desire for wealth, luxury, and ease decided to refrain from parenthood. Nor would he consider a woman's desire to escape the discomforts of pregnancy or to avoid its possible effect upon her attractiveness a valid reason for the use of birth control. One of the foremost proponents of the planned parenthood movement, Alfred Martin Rehwinkel, says, "To refuse beforehand therefore, and by design, to have any children although physically and mentally fit to have them would be a manifest violation of God's ordinance of marriage." [4] No consideration of the morality of birth control can be complete until the responsibility of the married to bear children is taken into account. The responsibility is far too serious to be overlooked

In seeking to determine when birth control is right and when it is wrong, the responsibility of parents to properly care for their children must be considered. Parenthood in its real meaning involves more than a biological process. There is more to being a parent than merely having a child. When a child comes into a home, along with the child comes the responsibility for his physical, mental, and spiritual nurture. Children are precious in the sight of God and he would not have them brought into the world to be unloved and neglected. Parenthood is a venture so serious that it dare not be entered into lightly or without serious thought. Leslie D. Weatherhead had this in mind when he said, "Parenthood ideally should be a responsible act rather than an accident of physical union." [5] Because of this responsibility which parents have to their children, conditions such as an economic crisis or poor parental health, which would make the fulfilment of this responsibility impossible, might dictate that parenthood be postponed

---

[4] *Planned Parenthood and Birth Control in the Light of Christian Ethics* (St. Louis: Concordia Publishing House, 1959), p. 99.

[5] *The Mastery of Sex Through Psychology and Religion* (Garden City: Blue Ribbon Books, 1932), p. 95.

for a time. Under such circumstances the practice of birth control would be right and moral.

By comparing and contrasting their responsibility to bear children and their responsibility to be proper parents to their children, a couple can go a long way toward determining whether birth control is right or wrong for them. However, let them remember that more than their own choice in the matter is involved. They must be able to justify their decision in the sight of God. Before they choose to use birth control, let them be certain that God will accept their reasons for doing so.

As the minister studies the controversial question of the morality of birth control, he will soon come to the conclusion that no categorical answer can be given to the question of whether the practice is right or wrong. For some couples it may be right and for others it may be wrong. It may be right for a couple at one time and wrong for them at another. In fact, this will almost always be the case, for only in a few rare instances would a couple be justified either in the permanent practice of birth control or in its permanent disuse.

If a couple feels that God would not have them become parents at the particular time when parenthood is under consideration, then they must practice some form of birth control in order to conform to his will. The practice of birth control for them is certainly moral, since by its use they are doing what they feel that God would have them to do. The method of its practice ceases to be the important thing and the motive behind its practice receives its true place of importance. If they are free to practice birth control at all, then they are free to practice it as effectively as current scientific discovery will allow. However, periodically they must ask themselves whether or not conditions have so changed that God now desires for them and will permit them the privilege of parenthood. If this is found to be the case, then the practice of birth control must be stopped. Never could the use of birth control be moral for the couple who feels that God would have them to become parents.

The minister confronted by a couple's question, "Is birth control right or wrong?" must lead them to see that there really is no answer to the question as they have stated it. In order to receive a valid answer, they must ask, "Is birth control right or wrong for us at this time?" Then the minister can aid them in the consideration of their responsibility to God for parenthood and in a consideration of possible valid reasons for the postponement of parenthood. He can help them find what they feel to be the will of God in the matter. Only in such a procedure can the controversial question as to the morality of birth control be rightly answered.

Additional Reading

BOVET, THEODOR. *Love, Skill and Mystery: A Handbook to Marriage.* Garden City, New York: Doubleday & Co., 1958.

COLACCI, MARIO. *Christian Marriage Today.* Minneapolis: Augsburg Publishing House, 1958.

FLETCHER, JOSEPH. *Morals and Medicine.* Princeton, New Jersey: Princeton University Press, 1954, pp. 65–99.

ROCK, JOHN, and LOTH, DAVID. *Voluntary Parenthood.* New York: Random House, 1949.

SULLOWAY, ALVAH W. *Birth Control and Catholic Doctrine.* Boston: Beacon Press, 1959.

5

The Right to Die

D. YATES BINGHAM

No one in this generation who deals with the processes of life and death in human relations can escape indefinitely the problem of voluntary euthanasia. When people suffer from "incurable" diseases that rend the heart, family and friends alike are often moved to question the wisdom of God in preserving life. Some Christians would seek to escape the problem by assigning it to the physician or the patient involved. Others would adopt the attitude that whatever is available to prevent suffering should be used, even to the extent of taking life. However, can the Christian find such easy relief from such an important problem of conscience?

What is a responsible Christian attitude in the area of euthanasia since human life is involved?

Euthanasia literally means an "easy death" but is generally known as "mercy killing." It is the deliberate easing into death of a patient suffering from a painful and fatal illness. The term in this setting involves only adults who request release from incurable suffering. The tremendous increase of malignant diseases is making these requests increasingly frequent.

While the majority of Christians hesitate in indecision concerning the problem, those who have decided in favor of the legality of euthanasia are busy trying to change the law to correspond to their feelings. Almost all literature which has been written is either by Catholics, who almost universally oppose the practice, or by those Protestants who favor it. There is an apparent need for a sane, conservative Christian approach to the problem. To provide a background for personal responsibility and decision, the subject of this chapter will be viewed from historical, legal, and moral perspec-

tives. The emphasis will be placed on individual Christian responsibility and individual decision.

A Historical Perspective

Euthanasia has been practiced in some form from the most
primitive times to the present day. Primitive societies currently
practice crude forms of euthanasia. In each instance the practice
seems to be associated with the value placed on human life in the
society. "One of the most noteworthy features of savage and barbarian,
as opposed to civilized, society is the relative unimportance of the
individual as compared with the community." [1] In such societies
human sacrifices shock no one, and the victim seems to accept the
procedure with calmness. Children are involved in the process as well
as adults and the aged. When the individual is of little or no usefulness
to his community, economic forces dictate the practice of elimination
for the sake of the group. The accompanying problem of suicide is
rare among uncivilized peoples, although it is known to exist.

In historical times the practice of euthanasia has been found in
varying degrees in many countries. On the whole, the Greeks
reverenced old age. Plato, however, seemed to be in accordance with
suicide when he took the position that it was justified in cases of
intolerable pain and disgrace. He also seemed willing to do away with
the inferior and the old. Stoic and Epicurean philosophers put a
premium on suicide, but of euthanasia nothing is said. Rome followed
the Stoic and Epicurean practices, which glorified suicide, and made
no particular variation in the practice.

Judaism and Christianity have a different conception of values to
that of other cultures. The Jewish value of the family and its members
leaves no room for the practice of euthanasia. Suicide was rare in Old
Testament times, though it was not formally prohibited. The higher
Judaistic concept of life, which set its face sternly against all forms of
self-destruction, was adopted and elevated by Christianity. From the
time of St. Augustine onward, the Sixth Commandment has been
regarded as covering suicide as well as murder and, therefore,
euthanasia.

The Christian value of the individual has been the legal and
traditional basis for physicians to keep a patient alive as long as

---

[1] H. R. Rose, "Euthanasia," *Encyclopaedia of Religion and Ethics*, ed. James
Hastings (12 vols; New York: Charles Scribner's Sons, 1914), V, 559.

possible. Christians have always accepted each individual as a creation of God and, therefore, worthy of individual care and consideration. There is a growing sentiment that this care should include the patient's right to choose the time of death when he is suffering from an incurable disease. Is this sentiment in harmony with the over-all Christian concept of life? Each Christian must seek an answer.

A Contemporary Problem

Voluntary euthanasia is a contemporary problem of the Christian conscience. Scientific progress in medicine, surgery, hygiene, and sanitation has lengthened one's life span by twenty years in a few decades, only to make more acute the dilemma of old age. The lengthened life span is accompanied by increasing incurable diseases. "The diseases increasingly confronting us today are those which are not acute or painless but prolonged and often painful. Each year, each day, our hospital facilities and all others for the care of the ill are more and more taxed to provide aid for those whose stay in bed will not be a week or a month but perhaps many months, and for whom there is no chance for any recovery." [2]

The greatest interest in voluntary euthanasia seems to stem from the desire to eliminate suffering. Scientific advances of medicine have brought an artificiality to human life that encourages even the individual Christian to shrink from the reality that the world is, indeed, sinful, and that sin brings suffering and death.

The rising sentiment to eliminate suffering as a contemporary problem has led to efforts to legalize euthanasia. Bills have been presented in two state legislatures, but both failed to pass. However, in 1948 a Gallup poll asked individuals the question, "When a person has a disease that cannot be cured, do you think doctors should be allowed by law to end the patient's life by some painless means if the patient and his family request it?" The question was answered as follows: 37 per cent, yes; 54 per cent, no; and 9 per cent, no opinion.[3] At that time the trend toward legalization of euthanasia was surprising, and there is little doubt but that it has been extended during more recent years.

---

[2] Howard Wilcox Haggard, "Why Legalize Voluntary Euthanasia." A tract prepared by the Euthanasia Society of America, 139 East 57th Street, New York 22, N. Y.

[3] "Mercy Killings," *Revelation*, XIX, No. 2, 53.

Another indication that euthanasia is a contemporary problem is that doctors overtly or permissively practice it. Dr. Ayer quotes from the May, 1948, issue of *Survey Graphic* as follows: "Perhaps the most amazing evidence of this was admission once drawn from a large gathering of physicians by Dr. Hugh Cabot, then consulting physician at Mayo Clinic, Rochester, Minn. At the close of an address on cancer, he made this startling request of his audience: 'Will those of you who have never put a hopelessly diseased patient out of his misery please raise your hand?' No one raised his hand." [4]

Although euthanasia is something most doctors do not discuss, two English doctors have admitted the practice, one in 1957 and the other in 1959. The first doctor appeared on television anonymously and admitted that he let two patients die "because he felt death more merciful than life." [5] He stated that he began the practice of euthanasia in his twenties without taking advice from other doctors. He said, "One cannot discuss such matters with anyone else. One has to make up one's own mind as an individual." The other doctor admitted that in the spring of 1959 he had given a patient the dose that would relieve her suffering. He explained that he had made the admission "to rebut arguments that there was no need of legislation giving doctors and their patients the right to reach an understanding in such tragic circumstances." [6] After the physician had been praised in the press, it was noted that the only difference between him and the average physician "is that the average doctor does not talk about such things."

Perhaps the most common form of "mercy killing" used by the Christian doctor is inaction. By omitting the use of medical means to prolong life when it has become a burden to the patient, the physician acts in a way that is conceded, even by Catholics, as moral. However, is this merely a willing justification which is not essentially different from the action of others? Whether this question is answered affirmatively or negatively, the fact that it seems to be a recognized practice among Christian physicians emphasizes the need for an ethical decision with regard to the problem.

------

[4] William Ward Ayer, "Can Christianity Countenance Mercy Killings?" *The Sunday School Times,* May 20, 1950, p. 435.

[5] "The Doctor Who Chose Death for Patients," *Newsweek,* July 8, 1957, p. 54.

[6] John Beavan, "The Patient's Right to Live, and Die," *New York Times Magazine,* August 9, 1959, p. 14.

The Legal Status of Voluntary Euthanasia

The legal status of voluntary euthanasia is based on the theological value of life. Fletcher, in condemning the theological influence, states that "the common civil law has always followed the line of the moral theologians." [7] He feels that such a practice is not necessarily the wisest or the best. However, it is the case.

Under the present law, voluntary euthanasia would, except in certain narrow circumstances, be regarded as suicide in the patient who consents and murder in the doctor who administers; even on a lenient view, most lawyers would say that it could not be less than manslaughter in the doctor, the punishment for which, according to the jurisdiction and the degree of manslaughter, can be anything up to imprisonment for life.[8]

The patient, of course, is freed from legal litigation in the case of suicide, but his life insurance company may refuse to pay off his policy. The physician's problem, however, is not so final.

The physician's predicament can be spelled out in clearer terms. He becomes a common murderer if he gives the patient a fatal injection with the intent to kill. If the physician furnishes poison to assist the patient to commit suicide, he is an abettor in the crime and is guilty of murder. A different circumstance is apparent when the physician administers a fatal dose which at the same time is the minimum necessary to deaden pain. This is termed by Catholics as "the principle of double effect," and is morally and legally justified in their opinion. Pope Pius XII supported this position when he said, "The removal of pain and consciousness by means of drugs when medical reasons suggest it is permitted by religion and morality to both doctor and patient even if the use of drugs will shorten life." Therefore, the physician's legal problem rests with the first two of these three circumstances.

There are four particular factors in administering the present law. Due to the nature of the evidence required, a charge against a physician for murder through the administering of a humane overdose is inherently difficult to establish. Furthermore, prosecuting authorities are reluctant to take criminal action against a physician of repute for

---

[7] Joseph Fletcher, *Morals and Medicine* (Princeton, N. J.: Princeton University Press, 1954), p. 180. Reprinted by permission.

[8] Glanville L. Williams, *The Sanctity of Life and the Criminal Law* (New York: Alfred A. Knopf, 1957), p. 318. Reprinted by permission.

an act done in good faith. Should the authorities prosecute, a jury is reluctant to convict a physician in these circumstances, and may act contrary to the judge's express legal direction. Should he even be convicted, in all probability executive clemency would intervene.

"There seems to be only one instance of the prosecution of a physician for mercy-killing either in the United States or in England. In 1949 a New Hampshire physician, Dr. Sander, dictated into the hospital record an admission to mercy-killing by the injection of air; on his trial he denied that his act had caused the patient's death, and this defense succeeded before the jury." [9] When the defendant has been a relative of the deceased rather than the physician, he has not always been treated so mercifully. Therefore, the prospect of a sentimental acquittal is not always certain.

The original Christian interpretation of the Sixth Commandment concerning the prohibition to take life is still the basis for legal action in many nations of the world.

Legislators know that there are no votes in law reform, but only votes to be lost through offending sectarian opinion. Moreover, legislators are themselves strongly affected by the traditional moral generalizations and taboos. Largely, perhaps, because of these facts, no country in the world has yet taken the step of legalizing voluntary euthanasia in fatal illnesses. The nearest approach is that made in Switzerland, which as already shown, allows the physician to put the poison into the patient's hand, though not to administer it himself. Norway, also, provides that the judge may reduce the punishment for mercy-killing below the minimum normally fixed by statute.[10]

With the growing leniency in the minds of many Christians and the leadership of the United States among the nations of the world, the legal action allowed by the present generation of Christians may affect the legalization of euthanasia in all parts of the world.

Attempts to Change the Present Law

There have been many attempts to change the present law. Many people feel that the present laws concerning euthanasia are inadequate and outmoded, and, therefore, should be changed. Whether the attitude toward change comes primarily from a more lenient translation of the Sixth Commandment, the individual's concern for the

[9] *Ibid.*, p. 328.
[10] *Ibid.*, p. 333.

physician, or the conception that the patient has the right to choose to die under certain circumstances, there are many supporters of new euthanasia legislation. These supporters include many Christian leaders who are usually found in the more liberal camp. Catholics, on the other hand, stand firmly against any change of legislation. Although a few conservative Protestants have spoken out against the proposed change, the majority seems to stand along the sidelines of the issue to observe rather than to act.

There has been an organized effort to change the law concerning euthanasia since 1936, when the English Euthanasia Society was formed. From its origin it has been supported by many physicians, public figures, and ministers of almost all denominations except Catholic. A bill was presented in the House of Lords in the same year. The object of the bill was to legalize voluntary euthanasia for anyone over twenty-one years of age who suffered from an incurable and fatal disease accompanied by severe pain. Although the bill lost by a small margin, it was introduced again in 1950, and was withdrawn after facing seemingly certain defeat. However, interest and support for the legislation in England has been publicized to the present time.

The Euthanasia Society of America, using the English Society as a model, was formed in 1938. Its first effort to legalize euthanasia was made that same year when a bill which it supported was introduced in the Nebraska legislature. Although the bill was defeated, the impact of the problem upon the American conscience had been initiated. By 1946, the society had formed in New York State a committee composed of 1,776 physicians and supported by 386 Protestant and Jewish ministers of religion.

A bill was prepared and presented to the New York State legislature, which was defeated. The nature of the bill is significant. It was based on the English bill and was permissive rather than mandatory. An involved system of checks was proposed to assure that euthanasia was available only to adults on a voluntary basis.[11] Fletcher sees this bill as a model for legislation. He describes it as follows:

It provides three things, essentially: (1) any sane person over twenty-one years old, suffering from an incurably painful and fatal disease, may

---

[11] For a fuller discussion of the actual bill, see Joseph V. Sullivan, *The Morality of Mercy-Killing* (Westminster, Md.: The Newman Press, 1950), pp. 23–28.

petition a court of record for euthanasia in a signed and attested document, with an affidavit from the attending physician that in his opinion the disease is incurable; (2) the court shall appoint a commission of three, of whom at least two shall be physicians, to investigate all aspects of the case and to report back to the courts whether the patient understands the purpose of his petition and comes under the provisions of the act; (3) upon a favorable report by the commission the court shall grant the petition, and *if it is still wanted by the patient* euthanasia may be administered by a physician or any other person chosen by the patient or by the commission.[12]

Others feel that the bill is too involved to be useful even should legislation be conscientiously admissible. However, the nature of the bill is significant, since it may be the first bill to be passed on the subject. Since 1947, the New York legislature has been petitioned by some group almost annually to pass the legislation.

Supporters of legalized euthanasia are not content to continue to work on the state level. In 1952, a petition, sponsored jointly by the United States and England, was presented to the United Nations in an effort to legalize euthanasia. Many influential names were among the 2,513 signatures on the petition. Although the petition failed to carry, the interest indicates that the controversial issue has sympathy in high places of influence. It also indicates that leaders of the movement are likely to become more vigorous as more interest is shown in the problem.

Are Christians with a conservative point of view going to stand idly by while those who have settled opinions change a law which tampers with the sanctity of life? Christian responsibility cannot be so easily relieved. Pastors and people alike need to make responsible decisions before America or the world awakens to find that the law has been changed while they slept.

Should the Law Be Changed?

The first decision which faces the Christian who seriously considers the problem of legalizing euthanasia is whether or not the law should be changed. This decision involves one's conception of tradition and principle, law and grace, man and God. Is the present law fixed by traditon or by principle? Is man completely under grace or is there a standard for action? What is the basis for decision—man's right or his

---

[12] *Op. cit.,* pp. 187–88.

responsibility to God? If law is merely the reflection of the changing mores of the people, then the criterion for change becomes the desire of the majority. Man's desire becomes the measure of all things, and law can be changed to reflect his purpose. This concept of man and law is dangerous from many points of view.

Man's moral responsibility becomes exceedingly important at this point. As a human being, man is a little lower than God, but he is not God. Maston says that "he should be seen as a human person, with all the limitations and weaknesses of the fleshly carnal nature, but at the same time as one with a divinely given potential." [13] This lofty concept leaves man subordinate to the moral will of God. Therefore, the moral law cannot change until God changes it. If man has previously misinterpreted God's will, the law should be changed to conform to his perfect will. Otherwise, it should remain as it is. A conclusion will be drawn by examining the moral aspects of the case both for and against voluntary euthanasia.

A Case for Voluntary Euthanasia

It is extremely difficult to delineate reason and moral responsibility when discussing the proposals of the protagonists of voluntary euthanasia. Being on the offensive, they hope to win the case by undermining the defense. The basis for argument is an interpretation of mercy as found in the Beatitudes (Matt. 5:7). Since the majority of people find it easy to accept the status quo, it may be wise to examine the offense in an attempt to decide what is *reason* and what is *responsibility,* and to examine the personal position of the individual in light of the findings.

The patient's inalienable right to die is of primary importance to the person who contends that voluntary euthanasia is justified.

In a very proper sense, the case for medical euthanasia depends upon the case for the righteousness of suicide, given the necessary circumstances. And the justification of its administration by an attending physician is therefore dependent upon it too, under the time-honored rule that what one may lawfully do another may help him to do. [14]

Fletcher equates the right to die with the hero who gives his life for a cause. He agrees with those who believe that the fatal sufferer "has the right to die, and that society should grant this right, showing the

---

[13] T. B. Maston, *Of One* (Atlanta: Home Mission Board, 1946), p. 69.
[14] Fletcher, *op. cit.,* p. 176.

same mercy to human beings as to the sub-human animal kingdom." Man is assumed to have the right to die because he is a personality. When personality ceases to function in freedom, knowledge, self-possession, and control, it is argued that life is prolonged uselessly.

Another argument for voluntary euthanasia which favors the patient is that physiological life is not sacrosanct. Man is accused of accepting life without the accompanying privilege of terminating it. "The Creator has given man reason, freedom, and conscience, and has left him with the possibility of ordering his own life within limits. He is to do the best he can with the material presented to him, and that means that it is the will of God that we should use our reason and conscience and our power to choose when we are faced with evils that have a remedy.[15]

According to this view, the individual should not be hampered by prejudices which would limit the full rights that he has to live or die, as he may wish. If he does, he is being directed by a form of vitalism or naturalistic determinism.

Perhaps the most sentiment-provoking argument for voluntary euthanasia is that the patient should be allowed to choose euthanasia rather than endure a degenerative death. All would agree that it is agonizing to see a loved one suffer when there is little or no hope for recovery. Conversely, this argument claims that to ask for euthanasia, to leave voluntarily for the unknown, would require faith, courage, and resolution. The great example of such resolution and courage is Charlotte Perkins Gilman, who was described as one of the twelve greatest American women. She chose self-euthanasia rather than endure the pains of cancer. Her last words, typed by her own hand just before she died, are these:

A last duty. Human life consists in mutual service. No grief, no pain, misfortune or "broken heart" is excuse for cutting off one's life while any power of service remains. But when all usefulness is over, when one is assured of an imminent and unavoidable death, it is the simplest of human rights to choose a quick and easy death in place of a slow and horrible one. Public opinion is changing on this subject. The time is approaching when we shall consider it abhorrent to our civilization to allow a human being to lie in prolonged agony which we should merci-fully end in any other creature. Believing this choice to be of social

---

[15] W. R. Matthews, "Voluntary Euthanasia, the Ethical Aspect," a pamphlet prepared by the Voluntary Euthanasia Legalisation Society of England.

service in promoting wiser views on this question, I have preferred
chloroform to cancer.[16]

Fletcher states that Miss Gilman's choice of self-euthanasia shows
"great wisdom and moral assurance." His statement is based on the
conclusion that her life had served its full usefulness, leaving no place
for regrets.

Some protagonists contend that legalization will protect the patient
from heirs or enemies who might use euthanasia to hasten death.
Fletcher states: "He would have far more protection than is provided
for many patients now committed for treatment of mental disorder.
He would, indeed, have a great deal more protection than he now
receives under the present system of clandestine euthanasia being
widely practiced." [17] This argument seems to question the ethics of the
physician as well as the enemies of the patient, and as such its validity
may be questioned.

Although the patient is most concerned with the right to die, the
case for voluntary euthanasia is equally concerned with the role of the
physician in the death. When the Hippocratic oath is discussed,
emphasis is placed on its "logical contradiction," which promises both
to relieve suffering and to prolong and protect life. Fletcher states that
"when the patient is in the grip of an agonizing and fatal disease, these
two promises are incompatible. Two duties come into conflict. To
prolong life is to violate the promise to relieve pain. To relieve the
pain is to violate the promise to prolong and protect life." [18] Due to
the law of diminishing returns which operates in narcosis, the
physician is often faced with the dilemma in incurable diseases of
either euthanasia or suffering.

Those who favor the practice of voluntary euthanasia say that it is
not murder when the physician co-operates, since the motivating force
is mercy rather than malice. Fletcher further states that "moralists
would contend that malice is not present as a motive in mercy-
killings; that they are mercy-aforethought, not malice-aforethought."
He continues in his attempt to justify his position by stating, "If we
can make no moral distinction between acts involving the same means,
then the thrifty parent who saves in order to educate his children is no

---

[16] Fletcher, *op. cit.*, p. 202.
[17] *Ibid.*, p. 207.
[18] *Ibid.*, p. 172.

higher in the scale of merit than the miser who saves for the sake of hoarding." Of course, this argument depends upon a definition of malice which does not correspond with the legal definition.

Perhaps the most dogmatic position taken by protagonists of voluntary euthanasia concerns the contention that the Sixth Commandment does not prohibit lawful killing. Fletcher assumes that both Catholics and "reactionary Protestants" reject his interpretation of the command. As the chief spokesman of his position, he states emphatically,

We might point out to the fundamentalists in the two major divisions of Western Christianity that the beatitude "Blessed are the merciful" has the force of a commandment too! The medical profession lives by it, has its whole *ethos* in it. But the simplest way to deal with this Christian text-proof objection might be to point out that the translation "Thou shalt not kill" is incorrect. It should be rendered, as in the responsive decalogue of the *Book of Common Prayer,* "Thou shalt do no murder," i.e., unlawful killing. . . . We might also remind the Bible-bound moralists that there was no condemnation either of Abimelech, who chose to die, or of his faithful sword-bearer who carried out his wish for him.[19]

Since Fletcher evidently feels that the major opposition against voluntary euthanasia stems from a misinterpretation of the commandment, his emphatic statements are more easily understood.

It is further argued that the physician, though fallible, rarely makes mistakes when life reaches the place of voluntary euthanasia. The competence and judgment of the physician must be trusted, or the doom of medical care is spelled. Williams states, "It may be allowed that mistakes are always possible, but this is so in any of the affairs of life. And it is just as possible to make a mistake by doing nothing as by acting. All that can be expected of any moral agent is that he should do his best on the facts as they appear to him." [20] Even when new cures are found for some diseases, advanced cases are rarely benefitted because physical deterioration and toxemia have already fatally damaged tissues and organs.

Another contention in the case for voluntary euthanasia is that physicians practice euthanasia with or without legal authority and, therefore, they should be relieved of legal responsibility. The physician

---

[19] *Ibid.,* pp. 195–96.
[20] *Op. cit.,* p. 318.

is well acquainted with methods of killing that leave no trace. These methods are practically impossible to prove. Williams says, "Provided that the act is expertly done and no unwise admissions made, the question of legal responsibility remains academic." However, it is contended that it places a psychological burden upon the physician. It is also contended that his decision is not one of life or death, but rather which kind of death, an agonized or peaceful one.

There is an underlying contention among the euthanasia supporters that those against euthanasia are inconsistent in their approach to life and death. "We are, by some strange habit of mind and heart, willing to impose death but unwilling to permit it: we will justify humanly contrived death when it violates the human integrity of its victims, but we condemn it when it is an intelligent voluntary decision. If death is not inevitable anyway, not desired by the subject, and not merciful, it is righteous! If it is happening anyway and is freely embraced and merciful, then it is wrong." [21] On the surface this accusation may seem valid. However, the basic principles concerning life, suffering, and death may lead to an entirely different point of view. These principles will be discussed in relation to the case *against* voluntary euthanasia.

A Case Against Voluntary Euthanasia

There is a divergence of backgrounds among those who oppose voluntary euthanasia. The Roman Catholic Church takes the firmest stand and has the loudest voice against it. However, there are other groups and individuals who are less organized but who take a common and a distinct position in the problem. It is the common ground between these groups which is now to be considered.

A basic argument against voluntary euthanasia is connected with the Sixth Commandment and the interpretation of the word "malice." It is generally conceded that the commandment does not forbid all killing, but only murder. However, murder legally involves malice. Can a person be deprived or relieved of his life without malice? Legally, he cannot. "Murder at common law is the voluntary taking of human life with malice aforethought, either expressed or implied. Malice here does not imply ill will. Any intentional killing of a human being without legal justification is stated to be malicious." [22] This

---

[21] Fletcher, *op. cit.*, p. 181.

[22] John F. Conlin, "Euthanasia, 'Unethical, Immoral,' " *Pastoral Psychology*, I (September, 1950), 35.

implies that voluntarily giving or taking life without a cause outside one's self is malicious and, therefore, sinful.

Sullivan states that "since man does not have full dominion over his own life, he obviously cannot give up a dominion he does not have." [23] The Catholic Church is very rigid in dealing with those who take their own lives and refuses them a Christian burial. Protestants are less adamant but usually hold that the action is extremely irregular. In either case, the basis for decision concerns God's control over the processes of life and death.

Another contention against voluntary euthanasia is that there must be a standard of action or else any action may be justified. Once a policy of expediency has been adopted, anything can be argued as being good which serves the desired purpose of the agent, whether state or individual. It is contended that there can no more be admitted mercy killing than mercy theft, mercy arson, or mercy embezzlement. Under such an expedient concept of morality, lying, cheating, and stealing can be viewed as legitimate means of promoting personal or general welfare.

The pessimistic effect upon the medical profession is a vital concern of some who stand against voluntary euthanasia. Ayer states that "it seems to a Christian minister that there is a danger that the practice could blight the high, godly basis of the medical profession itself." [24] New discoveries are being made daily which lengthen life and give renewed hope to sufferers.

A vivid instance of this comes to attention in the summer 1956 issue of *Your Radiologist*, bulletin of the American College of Radiology. Parents of a 27-day-old baby had been told that life-long idiocy was the child's fate. But in the course of a routine X-ray of the infant's chest, it was discovered by accident that his wrist-bones were not developing. Could it be that his skull was not developing properly, either, and that this accounted for the subnormal reactions? An X-ray of the head revealed just that, and the solution of the "idiocy" was at hand, because the thyroid gland regulates growth and "hormone boosters" could easily be administered to enable the skull and brain to develop.[25]

However, if euthanasia is legalized, people who are already fearful of

[23] Sullivan, *op. cit.*, p. 45.

[24] *Op. cit.*, p. 436.

[25] "One Stigma That Won't Beat a Dogma," *America*, September 15, 1956, p. 557.

the physician's capabilities may shrink from him in fear and anxiety at a time when they need his services most. Certainly, the scientific advancements of today should make it a time of great optimism rather than pessimism in the medical profession.

Some physicians, themselves, are opposed to legalized euthanasia because "it would put too great a responsibility upon them" and because "it is a doctor's business to cure, not to kill." Comparatively few physicians, excluding those of the New York committee, desire a change in the legal approach to the problem. The consensus of opinion seems to be that a thing which is intrinsically immoral cannot be made moral through legislation. "Doctors I have spoken to feel that they have no real difficulty in behaving in a compassionate and moral way, and need have no fear of legal consequences. Some of them say that legislation purporting to widen their professional freedom might actually reduce it, and would certainly diminish their personal responsibility to do what they think best for dying patients." [26]

The physician feels a moral responsibility to his profession and to his patient. He contends that he can fulfil both responsibilities conscientiously without legal intervention. Unless his patients and the public in general have equal respect for his ability, his professional usefulness will soon cease.

The "wedge principle" is a particularly strong argument against voluntary euthanasia. This principle "means that an act which, if raised to a general line of conduct, would injure humanity is wrong even in an individual case." Sullivan, who supports this principle, admits that individual cases may be justified but because of common danger there is a general prohibition.

Once a man is permitted on his own authority to kill an innocent person directly, there is no way of stopping the advancement of that wedge. There exists no longer any rational grounds for saying that the wedge can advance so far and no farther. Once the exception has been admitted it is too late; hence the grave reason why no exception may be allowed. That is why euthanasia . . . must be condemned.[27]

This principle recognizes the danger of compulsory euthanasia as the next step beyond legalized voluntary euthanasia. This danger seems to be justified by a statement distributed by the Euthanasia Society of

[26] Beavan, *op. cit.*, p. 22.
[27] *Op. cit.*, pp. 54–55.

America, which reads as follows: "While the Euthanasia Society's members are at present crusading for a bill to allow a sufferer to be put to death at his own request, they can foresee the day when it will be legally permissible to end the lives of acutely abnormal youngsters who are doomed to lead a useless existence." [28] No one can foresee where such freedom would eventually lead.

The eternal value of life must not be neglected in denying the moral justification of euthanasia. Does man have the supreme right of life, or does it belong to God? Has God abdicated his rulership of the world in favor of man? Regardless of the value of personality, the immutable laws of God are standard. God could not spare his own Son from suffering death in agony. Man, created in his own image and commended to his love, must likewise live and die according to divine law. "Man is a creature. He belongs to God. God's laws have been clearly set forth. Man has a right to use his life but does not possess the right of absolute disposal. The rights of God over life cannot be waived by patient, relative, physician, or state." [29] The sanctity of life is a hard-won achievement of Christian civilization, and once the position is compromised for any pragmatic reason, civilization will be on a slippery slope.

Pain and suffering are innate and natural in life. No one can completely escape them. However, mankind gladly accepts the blessings of life but shrinks from its burdens. Harkness has stated that "the price we pay for living in an orderly, law-abiding world is the possibility that suffering may sometimes be our lot." [30] The participation in life's gains must carry the necessity of sharing in its losses. Suffering can lead to a deeper fellowship with God; thus, it can be transcended. It can also teach observers of their need to depend completely upon God. Simply to be free from physical suffering is not the total answer.

Death, however, is another form of existence upon which only the Christian revelation speaks. Men may forget or reject God, but they cannot escape God by the grave. Neither can they be guiltless in attempting to

---

[28] "Taking Life Legally," reprinted from *Magazine Digest,* March, 1947, and distributed by Euthanasia Society of America, Inc., 139 East 57th Street, New York 22, N. Y.

[29] Conlin, *op. cit.,* p. 36.

[30] Georgia Harkness, *Conflicts in Religious Thought* (New York: Henry Holt & Co., 1929), p. 104.

do so, for innately, though often dimly, men know that God gave them existence and that he holds them responsible for their lives.[31]

Suffering is being largely eliminated from life through medical research. Perhaps the key to the solution is not in euthanasia but in endurance.

Conclusion

The problem of euthanasia will confront Christians as long as people suffer lengthy and deteriorating illnesses. Relativists probably will continue to use every effort to legalize a practice which is inherently questionable if not evil. What position should the Christian pastor take in this matter? What can he say? What should he do? The sidelines of the issue have become overcrowded, and both the pastor and the individual Christian are being forced to take a stand. Their chosen position must be delineated by some very basic Christian principles.

Personal suffering seems to be at the heart of the dilemma. There are few volunteers for suffering. It is a problem of nature which needs neither to be deified nor dignified. However, it must be accepted as a part of human existence. The Christian realizes that many who suffer most make a large contribution to the spiritual welfare of the community. Many "hopeless" cases have recovered and served useful purposes afterward. The time when sufferers cease to be useful is beyond the comprehension of the human mind. It must be left in the hands of God.

The example of Jesus teaches that personal authority should not be used for selfish purposes. Jesus had every human right, but he also recognized the adjoining responsibilities. He never used his human or divine authority for personal physical comfort or convenience. He never used expediency, but endured the necessary suffering that life and death entail, even to the cross. Paul challenged the Christian to a fellowship in self-denial and suffering when he said, "That I may know him and the power of his resurrection, and may share his sufferings, becoming like him in his death" (Phil. 3:10, RSV).

The responsibility of the individual conscience is another principle which the Christian must recognize in the physician's role in medical ethics. There are many twilight areas in medical practice where only

---

[31] *Revelation*, p. 75.

the physician can be responsible. He must decide between action and inaction for the good of the patient. These decisions should be made within legal bounds but without legal interference or problems of conscience. Too much legislation might create more problems in medical care than it would supposedly solve.

The ultimate criterion of voluntary euthanasia concerns the right of life and death. Has control been placed in the hands of man himself, or has God reserved it for himself alone? The answer to this question will determine the legality of voluntary euthanasia.

A satisfying answer to one who contemplates or seeks release through euthanasia is not found in the responses of the natural emotional sympathy with its medical, clerical, and psychological support; nor in the humanitarian logic of noble men with its sociological support; nor in the philosophical reasonings of the learned; nor in the opinion of the people. Whence, then, is the answer to be found? For the Christian it is simply stated in God's revelation. "Ye are not your own . . . ye are bought with a price: therefore glorify God in your body, and in your spirit, which are God's" (1 Cor. 6:19–20).[32]

---

[32] *Ibid.,* p. 76.

6

Capital Punishment

F. B. HUEY, JR.

"I believe in capital punishment, but, of course, I would not want to pull the switch that ends a man's life." This statement is typical of those who say that they believe in capital punishment. It indicates a basic inconsistency, because conviction concerning a principle should result in a desire for total participation in putting the principle into practice.

The defender of capital punishment may be resting his hand more heavily on the death switch than he realizes. As a voter, his hand helps pull the switch every time a person is executed, because voters in a democracy can change the laws if they really desire change. If laws are right, no citizen should hesitate to help carry them out. If they are wrong, he should be equally vigorous in his efforts to have them changed. If the laws enforcing capital punishment are wrong, then the voting citizens have committed murder by proxy every time the death switch is pulled.

The question of capital punishment is an issue of international importance. The State Department's intervention with its influence to stay the execution of Caryl Chessman of California for fear of international repercussions was evidence that abolitionists are not to be categorized with those "harmless" crusaders in behalf of antivivisection, vegetarian diets, or yogi exercises. The issue was brought to the fore of international consideration when representatives of Sweden, Austria, Ceylon, Uruguay, Ecuador, and Venezuela called on the United Nations to underwrite a study of capital punishment with a view to its universal abolition.

The rightness or wrongness of capital punishment must be faced squarely by every conscientious and law-abiding citizen. Those who have accepted its rightness without careful analysis need to rethink their position objectively.

A History of Capital Punishment

Capital punishment, the penalty of death for various offenses pronounced by a competent court, has its roots embedded deeply in man's culture, even back to the shadowy dawn of civilization. Its history shows a shifting emphasis from sacrilege and offenses against property to murder, to which it is largely limited today.

The ancient laws of Hammurabi were somewhat indiscriminate in providing the death penalty. A wife could sue her husband for legal separation, but if it could be proved that the marriage failure was her fault, she was to be drowned. If a contractor built a house so carelessly that it resulted in the death of the owner's son, the builder's son was put to death. This principle of *lex talionis* was enforced to the point of cutting off a hand that struck a father or cutting off both hands of an unskilful surgeon who might make a mistake.

The ancient Hebrews inflicted the death penalty on the person who cursed his father or mother, broke the sabbath, or was guilty of witchcraft. For the Roman, murder was punishable by death, but so was forgery by slaves. In Anglo-Saxon times murder was punished only by a fine, two thirds of which went to the relatives and one third to the king.

Some of these ancient laws seem mild in comparison to laws of England as recently as 1800, when around 250 offenses were punishable by death, from the stealing of a turnip to the cutting down of a tree. In 1801, a thirteen-year-old child was hanged for stealing a spoon, and children as young as seven were not spared the hangman's noose.

Reformers in England met with vigorous opposition from those in high places. In 1820, the lord chancellor opposed the removal of the death penalty for cutting down a tree. The sagacious lord voiced his concern thus: "It did undoubtedly seem a hardship that so heavy a punishment as that of death should be affixed to the cutting down of a single tree . . . but . . . if the Bill passed . . . a person might root up or cut down whole acres of plantations." [1]

This same concern was expressed by the chief of justice in 1810,

---

[1] Gerald Gardiner, *Capital Punishment as a Deterrent, and the Alternative* (London: Victor Gollancz, 1956), pp. 28–29.

when abolition of the death penalty for shoplifting was being considered. He said, "Were the terror of death . . . to be removed . . . shops would be liable to unavoidable losses from depredations . . . and bankruptcy and ruin must become the lot of honest and laborious tradesmen." [2] The learned judge visualized that whole stores would be stripped to the bare walls by criminals no longer terrorized by the threat of death.

It should not be concluded that capital punishment is always administered more judiciously in this enlightened age. In 1950, Jimmy Wilson, a Negro, was sentenced by Alabama law to die in the electric chair. His crime was the stealing of one dollar and ninety-five cents from a white woman. Only a storm of protest caused the sentence to be commuted.

Advocates of capital punishment are inconsistent at the point of the enforcement of law. Most would agree that the above cited case should not have been given the death penalty and yet quote the Bible as evidence that the present laws should never be changed. To prove that the New Testament does not support change in laws to make them more lenient, Vellenga has quoted Romans 13:1. [3] If his argument were valid, men would still be living under the tyranny of laws in effect in the days of Nero, and England would never have changed her laws which were in force a century ago. Children seven years of age could still be hanged for stealing a turnip.

Vellenga also quoted Romans 13:2–4, as proof that no one should meddle with the laws of the land against wrongdoing. It is a poor exegesis of the Scriptures that would take the idea of "resist not" to say that the citizenry cannot go through legal processes to change the laws when they are wrong and unjust.

Arguments for Capital Punishment

A major rational argument for capital punishment is that it is a greater deterrent to crime than any other form of punishment. Logically, such reasoning would conclude that its abolition would result in increase of murder. However, statistics have always proved that abolition does not cause an increase in crime. Defenders of capital punishment never deny the figures. They either ignore them, say that

---

[2] *Ibid.*, p. 25.
[3] Jacob J. Vellenga, "Is Capital Punishment Wrong?" *Christianity Today,* IV (October 12, 1959), 8.

statistics lie or do not prove anything, or that past experience would not hold in the present situation. The defenders of capital punishment have produced no figures to substantiate their position of its deterrent value.

The facts are that Denmark, Finland, Belgium, Norway, Austria, Sweden, and Switzerland abolished capital punishment, and the murder rate did not go up or down. England suspended the death penalty for seven months in 1948. During this period the average number of murders per month was eleven and one half. The following month, when the death penalty was reinstated, the number of murders was twenty-five. Actually, crime was more rampant in Britain during the period when the death penalty was invoked most liberally. The crime rate declined there when Scotland Yard became an effective agency for sending men to prison. When the penalty of death was abolished for forgery in England in 1836, the number of convictions for that crime decreased—contrary to the gloomy predictions which had been made. Nor did the crime rate increase when the death penalty was lifted for defacing the Westminster Bridge and for picking of pockets.

The quotation from Job, "All that a man hath will he give for his life" (2:4), has been invoked as proof text for the deterrent value of capital punishment. When it is remembered that Satan is the author of this statement, his opinion as a competent authority cannot be accepted.

Since one third of all murderers commit suicide after committing their crime, the fear of the death penalty serves as no deterrent to them. Since 80 to 90 per cent of all murders are committed by the insane or those who kill in sudden passion or while inebriated, the death penalty is no deterrent to them. It is not a deterrent to the person who thinks he can commit the perfect crime. This would leave it only as a deterrent for the professional criminal, and statistics give evidence that murder is mainly a crime of amateurs, not professionals.

Actually, the press sensationalism connected with a murder trial seems to serve as an incentive rather than as a deterrent. Crimes read about in the newspapers are duplicated. The publicity appeals to some. One murderer, on seeing the account of his deed in the newspaper, said, "I felt that at last I was somebody."

Another argument advanced for holding to capital punishment is that more policemen would be killed if the death penalty were abolished. Professor Thorsten Sellin of the University of Pennsylvania made a survey which proved that there was no more killing or wounding of policemen in six states with no death penalty than in the bordering death-penalty states.

It is also argued that there is no satisfactory alternative punishment to a life for a life. Opponents answer that the chief deterrent to crime is not the severity of punishment but the certainty of conviction. It is a well-known fact that only a small per cent of those guilty of crimes punishable by death are executed each year.

Abolitionists claim that imprisonment is a sufficient purgatory and that in prison the person can be rehabilitated. The only rational approach to crime is the clinical or curative approach. The number of released murderers who commit the same crime again is infinitesimal. This is contrary to the popular picture that they are biding their time, just waiting for the day to get out to get even with all who had a part in their conviction.

To argue that imprisonment lets a person off too lightly has a vengeful sound, but the argument of retribution is often advanced by supporters of capital punishment who say one ought to lose his life if he takes the life of another. If capital punishment is an instrument of retribution, it must satisfy a popular demand in a way no other punishment could. Whether it is right or necessary for the state to encourage its satisfaction should be considered. It has even been argued that it is less expensive to kill a man than to keep him in prison for life. Woodrow Wyatt answers, "This argument is wicked and immoral. Are we to kill men and women in cold blood because it is too expensive to maintain a prison in which to house them?" [4]

Some argue against imprisonment from the opposite viewpoint. They say that the sentence of imprisonment for life is worse than death. To hold this view one should logically conclude that we ought to reprieve those we now hang and hang those we now reprieve.

It is argued that public opinion demands the continuance of capital punishment, but popular opinion is not a good guide to determine whether it should be abolished or not. Polls have been made after an unusually repellent murder has stirred public opinion and the number in favor of the death penalty skyrockets, but in those cases where the public is in sympathy with the accused, opinion just as quickly goes

---

[4] "Again the Issue of Capital Punishment," *New York Times,* January 8, 1956, p. 44.

the other way. It was the hanging of attractive Ruth Ellis in England several years ago that set the abolitionist movement in full swing, because public sympathy was on her side, even though her guilt was clearly established.

Arguments Against Capital Punishment

In 1764, Cesare Beccaria first assailed the death penalty in his book *On Crimes and Punishments*. He argued that the death penalty should be abandoned because it infringed natural law and the social compact; because it was unnecessarily severe; because it brutalized the state; because it barbarized the citizenry; because it was more likely to inspire than to prevent crime; and that the chance of error constitutes of itself a sufficient reason for abolishing it. His book was accepted by Adams, Jefferson, and Madison in the United States, and his basic arguments against capital punishment are still advanced today.

It is true that executions have brought out the worst in men. When hangings were publicly held in England, they were occasions for great revelry. The working man looked forward to his few holidays during the year—Christmas, Easter, and the eight hanging days. Even men in high places have shown their brutality in this matter of taking a life. The famous Sir Edward Coke said hanging was not enough; the convicted criminals should not only be hanged but cut in pieces. He quoted the Bible in support of his position.

Blackstone, the eminent jurist whose textbooks are the standard reference books of lawyers today, also favored the drawing and quartering of the hanged man. He concurred in the practice of the day—hanging the corpse of the criminal in chains on a gibbet on the English roadside, as it was a "comfortable sight to the relations and friends" of the murdered person.

Archdeacon William Paley believed in capital punishment and recommended that some criminals should be thrown in the cages of wild animals to be torn apart and devoured.

The aged British man of letters of a few years ago, George Bernard Shaw, advocated not only the execution of the hardened criminal but also the subnormal man. His vicious attitude was expressed in these words, "The ungovernables, the ferocious, the conscienceless, the idiots, the self-centered myopes, and morons, what of them? Do not punish them. Kill, kill, kill, kill, kill them." [5]

---

[5] "Capital Punishment," *Atlantic Monthly*, vol. 181 (June, 1948), p. 52.

The fact that an average of five applications a week are made for the post of hangman in England reveals qualities of a sort that no state should wish to see cultivated in its citizens. Perhaps it is true that "though we loathe the criminal and the hangman, we harbor some part of each within us." [6]

Another argument used against capital punishment is the possibility of the occasional execution of an innocent person. Benjamin Franklin and Lafayette said that as long as there is any chance for human fallibility, no one should be executed. Koestler argues that judicial errors are not rare but are rarely detected. He believes that there is the probability of error inherent in the judicial procedure because of the possibility that witnesses can make mistakes. Handwriting and blood experts can be and have been wrong. There is the possibility of coincidence which can weave a web of circumstantial evidence around an innocent person. The fallibility of juries and judges and the carelessness of lawyers, especially in the cases of those unable to pay legal fees for their defense, also can spell error. It has been estimated that the number of condemnations of innocent persons runs as high as 5 per cent. To argue that it is not possible for man to make a mistake when it comes to taking the life of another is to forget that it was man who condemned and took the life of the Son of God.

It is also argued that to take the life of another is morally wrong. It must be remembered that the Christian purpose is redemptive. The Christian message is that no one is beyond the reach of spiritual reclamation. Capital punishment is a denial of this basic Christian principle. The spirit of Christianity is completely missed by one who would say, "If a wanton killer does not repent when the sentence of death is upon him, he certainly will not repent if he has 20 to 50 years of life imprisonment ahead of him." [7]

William Temple wisely suggested that it is always immoral to treat a person only as a means to some end other than his own well-being. By no stretch of the imagination could it be argued that the infliction of the death penalty results in a person's well-being.

It is also argued that it is wrong to continue a punishment which deprives a man of any ability to rectify a mistake, which, being human, he may make. Investigation of prison records would show that our

---

[6] Victor C. Ferkiss, "A Life for a Life," *The Commonweal*, LXIII (October 7, 1955), 12.

[7] Vellenga, *op. cit.*, p. 9.

modern prison system does bring about rehabilitation of many and makes them useful members of society.

A forceful argument against capital punishment is that there is no other form of punishment which imposes so much suffering on wholly innocent people. Granted that capital punishment is right for the offender, what about the agony and stigma that come upon his family through no fault of their own? Surely no one would argue that the family of the offender deserves to suffer in the way that they surely must when the death penalty is invoked.

The horrors of legal execution provide another reason for its abolition, although some might not concede this to be a major argument. The condemned is often subjected to unmentionable indignities by those who witness his death, even in a day when public executions have been abolished.

No form of legal execution is as totally quick and "painless" as its advocates maintain. Failures, delays, and mistakes have written a grisly chapter in the history of capital punishment. It is often a nightmare to those who must witness it. In England, where hanging was the prescribed method of legal execution, one woman's insides fell out as she went through the trap. All those who witnessed the scene suffered various degrees of damage to their nervous systems. There, where hanging was practiced until capital punishment was abolished, the body was never turned over to the family for burial but was buried in the prison courtyard.

A final argument against capital punishment is that respect for human life is best inculcated by the state itself refraining from taking life in the name of the law. Archbishop William Temple said that if the state held life sacred, it would express this belief better by refusing to take life under any circumstances than by taking it to prevent others from doing so. A paradox here is that both sides base their case on the sanctity of the individual. One lays stress on the sanctity of the life of the murderer, the other on his victim.

What the Scriptures Say

All the arguments presented thus far on both sides have been rational arguments. Ultimately, the Christian must be guided by what the Scriptures say. Some Scripture references are not understandable by the application of logic, but they are accepted. If the Scriptures clearly command capital punishment, the Christian's position would have to be acquiescence, all other arguments notwithstanding. He could not argue as did Charles Dickens, "If any text appeared to justify the claim [for capital punishment], I would reject that limited appeal."

Gowers has suggested that fundamentally each side takes its stand on dogma. On the one side is the dogma that it is "right" that one who takes life should forfeit his own. On the other side is the dogma that it is "wrong" that the state should take life. He calls these the Old Testament and New Testament dogmas.

The advocates of capital punishment make their strongest scriptural appeal from the Old Testament. For example, "Whoso sheddeth man's blood, by man shall his blood be shed: for in the image of God made he man" (Gen. 9:6). The problem with this kind of appeal to the Old Testament is the same one the Jews had when they were confronted with Christianity. They wanted to put new wine in old skins. Jesus came to fulfil the Law in the sense of filling it full of meaning for those who had so sadly misinterpreted it. He did not come to make Old Testament law binding upon his followers, in the sense of making them bound by its ritual and laws, but to bring to completion all to which the Old Testament had pointed.

Paul was confronted with the law-versus-grace issue, as will be all Christians through all the centuries. The conservative who accuses another of the "scissors and paste" method of dealing with certain passages of Scripture finds himself with scissors in hand at this point, as he claims Genesis 9:6 to be still binding. But he readily acknowledges that other Old Testament laws are not binding. The Old Testament included many other crimes for which the death penalty was compulsory. The book of Exodus required the death penalty for striking one's father or mother (21:15); stealing and selling a man (21:16); cursing one's father or mother (21:17); and it required the execution of witches (22:18). Leviticus added adultery as a capital offense (20:10). To be consistent, if one claims as binding Genesis 9:6, he must handle other Old Testament passages the same way.

To claim that this passage is a universal law not abrogated may sound weighty, but it has no basis in fact. If the Scofield dispensational interpretation were followed, Genesis 9:6 would be a part of the Noachian covenant. No claim is made by proponents of this method of interpretation that any of the other covenants is binding (Edenic, Adamic, Abrahamic, Mosaic, Palestinian, and Davidic), so it is difficult to understand why many of them maintain that Genesis 9:6 is still binding.

It is sad that sometimes an unrelenting, unforgiving spirit is found among conservative and fundamentalist Christians, and a passage like Genesis 9:6 is held to with vengeful delight. This spirit could lead one to make the following statement and see no anomaly in it: "Why not really be Christian and let the authorities put to death those unfitted for society while we place our sympathies where they belong?" [8]

Granting that Genesis 9:6 is still binding, the command was not given to the secular state, and to insist that this function should be carried out by the state is to affirm murder by proxy.

However, the ultimate basis of the death penalty in Genesis 9:6 was not civil in the narrow modern sense of serving the maintenance of order in society or the punishment of the guilty. It was expiatory. Life is God's peculiar possession which man may not profane at will. As expressed clearly by Yoder,

Thus the function of capital punishment in Genesis 9 is not the defense of society but the expiation of an offense against the Image of God. If this be the case then—and both exegetical and anthropological studies confirm strongly that it is—then the central events of the New Testament, the Cross and the Resurrection, are overwhelmingly relevant to this issue. The sacrifice of Christ is the end of all expiatory killing; only an unbiblical compartmentalization can argue that the event of the Cross, itself a typical phenomenon of miscarried civil justice issuing in the execution of an innocent, has nothing to do with the civil order.[9]

Another Scripture reference used by the advocate of capital punishment says, "Eye for eye, tooth for tooth, hand for hand, foot for foot" (Ex. 21:24). However, this same book from which this text is taken prescribes death for working on the sabbath and for cursing one's father and mother.

In order to interpret this seemingly severe maxim correctly, it is necessary to understand the age in which it was given. Capital punishment was the accepted practice of primitive communities. So imbued were men with the idea of taking another's life that their laws were quite severe. It is said that the laws of ancient Greece were

---

[8] Ernest Beam, "Correspondence," *The Christian Century*, LII (June 26, 1935), 857.

[9] John Howard Yoder, "Capital Punishment and the Bible," *Christianity Today*, IV (February 1, 1960), 5.

written in blood. Draco, the traditional lawgiver of earlier Greece, expressed the attitude of the age when he said that even the smaller crimes should be punished by death. Therefore, the Hebrew criminal legislation represented a distinct advance over the prevailing codes of other nations. The so-called *lex talionis,* "an eye for an eye," was in reality not a law of vengeance but of equivalence. The Mosaic statutes provided for a proportionate or equivalent infliction—an eye for an eye rather than a life for an injury. Humanity was on its way to a higher order of social procedure which would one day find its culmination in the ethics of Jesus. As he taught that the supreme obligation of the individual or a society toward the offender is forgiveness, it must have sounded strange to ears accustomed to the cry for revenge.

It is improper exegesis not to consider the New Testament teachings in relation to those of the Old Testament. Jesus came to fulfil the Law—to go beyond the understanding those of his day had of it. However, it is not necessary to turn to the New Testament to find these evidences of God's true attitude toward man. In the same section requiring death for various offenses is this statement, "Thou shalt not avenge, nor bear any grudge against the children of thy people, but thou shalt love thy neighbour as thyself" (Lev. 19:18). This statement must be weighed carefully in the total picture, "As I live, saith the Lord God, I have no pleasure in the death of the wicked; but that the wicked turn from his way and live" (Ezek. 33:11). Perhaps no Old Testament writer so fully understood the love of God as did Hosea. He came to understand this love through the bitter personal experience with a wayward wife. Having forgiven her because of an intense love, he could understand the throbbing heart of God, as he said, "I will not execute the fierceness of mine anger, I will not return to destroy Ephraim; for I am God, and not man" (Hosea 11:9).

If the Pentateuch alone is to be taken as the final guide, there is at least one occasion when divine disapproval of capital punishment was indicated, even for the crime of murder. Cain committed the first murder, but rather than putting him to death, God branded him to protect him lest anyone finding him might slay him.

If one's appeal is to the Old Testament it must be conceded that there is not unequivocal proof that capital punishment was always God's remedy for the offender. The person who believes in a life for a life will probably feel that the issue is settled and that the New

Testament could have nothing to say that would modify his beliefs. However, Jesus dealt quite specifically with this concept when he said, "Ye have heard that it hath been said, An eye for an eye, and a tooth for a tooth: But I say unto you, That ye resist not evil: but whosoever shall smite thee on thy right cheek, turn to him the other also" (Matt. 5:38–39).

Does this statement mean that Jesus was contradicting a law given by God? Not at all. It was simply another indication of the fulfilment of the Law by Jesus. He could make this statement because he was to pay the penalty for sins. It was his life given for any other life.

Jesus made it clear that men had misinterpreted the Law. On at least two occasions he summarized its true intent. Once he said, "Therefore all things whatsoever ye would that men should do to you, do ye even so to them: for this is the law and the prophets" (Matt. 7:12). It would be difficult for a sane person to advocate capital punishment for another if guided by this principle. Another time he summarized the Law by stating that man was to love God unreservedly and his neighbor as himself. He concluded by saying, "On these two commandments hang all the law and the prophets" (Matt. 22:40). By no stretch of the imagination could a person obey the spirit of these commandments and recommend the death penalty for his neighbor. These words of Jesus cannot be ignored if one is to arrive at a proper interpretation of the Old Testament teachings, which, at first glance, seem to warrant punishment.

The only direct reference to capital punishment in the New Testament is found in the eighth chapter of John's Gospel and should be noted. A woman had committed an offense punishable by death under the Mosaic code. There was no doubt about her guilt. The leaders intended to put Jesus on the spot in this situation, and, therefore, they must have suspected that he would disagree with the Law. Jesus did not deny that capital punishment for the offense of adultery was part of the Mosaic code, but he brought two other matters to bear on the situation. He first raised the issue of the moral authority of the judge and executioner when he stated, "He that is without sin . . . let him first cast a stone" (John 8:7). He then exercised his right to forgive her sin. Forgiveness in such a spirit as this becomes the Christian imperative.

The New Testament concept of human relationships is the law of love. This is expressed succinctly in 1 John 3:18; 4:12, 20, and by the apostle Paul, who said, "Love worketh no ill to his neighbour: therefore love is the fulfilling of the law" (Rom. 13:10). The idea that men could kill a fellowman's body while loving his soul is impossible, for love considers the total well-being of another person.

When the runaway slave Onesimus decided to return to his master after having become a Christian, he knew that as an escaped slave, under Roman law, he was subject to punishment, including death, if the owner desired. Paul wrote a letter to the owner requesting mercy for Onesimus to the degree that he would receive the slave as a brother, as though he were Paul himself.

Paul also reminded those who felt that God had given over to man the prerogative of judgment and the taking of a life that even under the Old Testament law this was not so. He quoted Deuteronomy 32:35 to the Christians at Rome as he exhorted them, "Dearly beloved, avenge not yourselves, but rather give place unto wrath: for it is written, Vengeance is mine; I will repay, saith the Lord" (Rom. 12:19). Men and society corrupt themselves indelibly when they assume this prerogative which God has clearly stated that he retains for himself. Jesus warned of the seriousness of judging others in Matthew 7:1–5.

Those advocating the abolition of capital punishment are not denying personal responsibility or assuming that the idea of sin and its subsequent retribution would be lessened or eliminated by a more humane treatment of the offenders. Instead, they recognize that the very essence of Christianity is to reform or change human life. As long as there is life, there is hope, but when the irreversible judgment of death is invoked by man, that chance, be it ever so slight, is obliterated for eternity.

Though not a determinative argument, it is interesting to note the positions taken by the various churches concerning capital punishment. Most of the major churches, with the notable exception of the Roman Catholic Church, deplore the use of the death penalty. Some have never taken an official stand on the matter.

The Methodist Church's stand against capital punishment has been part of its discipline since 1940. It reads: "We stand for the application of the redemptive principle to the treatment of offenders against the law, to reform of penal and correctional methods, and to criminal court procedure. For this reason, we deplore the use of capital punishment."

The United Presbyterian Church in the United States of America went on record in its General Assembly in 1959 as "believing that capital punishment cannot be condoned by an interpretation of the Bible based upon the revelation of God's love in Jesus Christ."

The General Convention of the Protestant Episcopal Church, in 1958, resolved that "the taking of this human life is within the providence of God and not within the right of man."

In view of the appeal to the Old Testament made by many in support of capital punishment, it is interesting to observe that many Jewish congregations are opposed to capital punishment. The Union of American Hebrew Congregations recently passed a resolution at their General Assembly which stated, "There is no crime for which the taking of human life by society is justified." In at least this one matter the modern Jew has repudiated the Pharisees among his forefathers who interpreted the Law so uncompromisingly.

The Canadian Catholic Conference, an agency of the Roman Catholic bishops of Canada, recently reiterated the Catholic position: "When a criminal endangers the common good by evil-doing, the state has the right to put him to death, if necessary." [10] The Catholic Church has been an avid supporter of capital punishment, especially for those who have refused allegiance to the Catholic Church. Its role of executioner, where it has been powerful enough to serve in the dual role of church and state, has written a bloody chapter in history.

In Retrospect

There is no conclusive proof that capital punishment does not serve as a deterrent, and crime does not increase where it has been abolished. Thorsten Sellin's careful study leaves no doubt at this point.[11] The brutal attitudes that are reflected by those who advocate capital punishment should cause them to examine their own motives for defending the practice. Is their defense based upon a sense of justice and rightness, or is it the natural man breaking through the veneer of the civilized man, delighting in wreaking vengeance and inflicting injury on another? One should not dismiss this charge too lightly.

[10] Tom Henshaw, "Churches Argue Capital Penalty," *Denton Record-Chronicle,* February 29, 1960, p. 5.

[11] Thorsten Sellin (ed.), "Murder and the Penalty of Death," *The Annals of the American Academy of Political and Social Science,* 284 (November, 1952).

To appeal to the Bible as a defense has been shown to be a misplaced emphasis and an untenable exegesis. To hold to part of the Law under previous covenants as still binding is simply a reflection of the age-old struggle between Judaism's representing the Law and Christianity's representing grace. Christ clearly taught that the fulfilment of the law is love—love for God and for one's fellowman. It is a love which requires forgiveness; a faith which believes that total transformation is possible, even for the most depraved person as long as there is a breath of life in him; and a hope that leaves vengeance in the hands of God, knowing that one day he will set it right.

Toward a Solution

The abolitionist is not minimizing the seriousness of the sin of murder in advocating elimination of the death penalty. His contention is that punishment should be both positive and reformative. This concept is in keeping with the New Testament teaching, "For whom the Lord loveth he chasteneth, and scourgeth every son whom he receiveth" (Heb. 12:6). God's punishment of his children is for their well-being, even as human fathers must exercise chastisement for the well-being of their offspring. This is a principle the state could well follow in fitting the punishment to the crime.

It is not the purpose of this author to offer specific terms of imprisonment for various crimes; that is a matter for the legal profession to work out. It seems that a step in the right direction is to consider the results in those nations which have substituted life imprisonment for the death penalty. A careful study was made by the Select Committee of 1930 in thirty-six countries or states where the death penalty was abolished. Their conclusion was that prolonged examination of the situation in those countries gives assurance that capital punishment may be abolished without endangering life or property or impairing the security of society.

A penalty of less than life imprisonment should be seriously considered, since it seems that many murderers can become useful citizens again after a period of imprisonment. As has been previously pointed out, most murderers are insane or momentarily crazed. If insane they need to be committed to an institution either for life or until pronounced cured by competent medical authorities. If the murder is an act of sudden passion, it has been found that this type is easier to reform than any other type of criminal.

Some argue that to release a murderer is unsafe, for he will commit the same crime again. The fact is that most reprieved murderers do not commit murder again because this crime is not usually the result of a "criminal class." As evidence for this contention, in England, 1928–48, 112 of 174 "lifers" were released. Only one of these, a man named Rowland, was ever alleged to have committed a second murder and was hanged. However, another man confessed to being the real murderer, but the government refused to reopen the case and went ahead and executed Rowland. Four years later the second man attempted an exact repetition of the first murder.

A reasonable prison sentence is a purgatory which no one can imagine who has not been there. The worst thing is being deprived of the right to be the master of one's destiny and of being under constant observation. It is a time which allows for repentance and for taking steps toward the reintegration of the individual into society.

The cross of Jesus Christ and the love and forgiveness of God which the cross represents must stand once and for all time as a barrier against one man's taking the life of another. Certainly, it is not easy to forgive one who has taken the life of another, especially if one is personally involved, but the challenge of Christian faith has never been easy. The ultimate example was expressed when the innocent one hanging on the cross said, "Father, forgive them." Because this is the spirit of Christ, Victor Hugo was right when he predicted that one day "the cross shall displace the scaffold."

The question of capital punishment is not an imaginary issue but one which vitally affects every person. If capital punishment is wrong rationally and cannot be defended under New Testament principles of human relations, then to permit it to continue places a responsibility upon every Christian voter who could exercise his influence to have this law removed from the statute books. Until he does, he must live with a troubled conscience that he has had his hand on the executioner's switch as surely as if he were present at the execution—a murderer by proxy.

Additional Reading

CLARK, GORDON H., MILLIGAN, CHARLES S., and YODER, JOHN HOWARD. "Capital Punishment and the Bible," *Christianity Today,* IV (February 1, 1960), 347–54.

"Death Penalty Must Go," *The Christian Century,* LXXIV (April 3, 1957), 413–14.

FERKISS, VICTOR C. "A Life for a Life," *The Commonweal,* LXIII (October 7, 1955), 12–15.

GOWERS, SIR ERNEST. *A Life for a Life?* London: Chatto & Windus, 1956.

KOESTLER, ARTHUR. *Reflections on Hanging.* New York: The Macmillan Co., 1957.

LEWIS, PETER E. "Capital Punishment," *Encyclopaedia Britannica,* IV (1958), 809–10.

SELLIN, THORSTEN (ed.). *The Annals of the American Academy of Political and Social Science.* November, 1952.

7

Christians Face the Race Problem

STANLEY O. WHITE

A pastor was enjoying a visit with some of the members of his church. The hosts were kind enough to invite him to spend these moments in the shade of a tree in the front yard where a slight breeze provided some relief from the summer heat. This was a rural community and such hospitality was typical. During the visit, several automobiles passed by. One of them became significant. As this particular automobile passed, the pastor raised his hand to greet the passer-by. The significance came when the lady of the house said, "Didn't you know that was a Negro when you waved?" The pastor replied, "I guess I noticed, but I really didn't think much about it."

The visit soon came to an end and the preacher went on his way. He left with some questions in his mind. "Why is it that any group of human beings should look down upon or ignore any other group of human beings? Why should anyone, especially Christians, think it unusual for a white man to greet a Negro? What's behind all of this anyway?" The preacher had thought little about these things before, but now he felt he must.

The time has come when many other Christians must consider these questions along with this pastor. The present race problem in the United States has been described as one of the most baffling and most difficult of all contemporary problems. Some say that certain racial groups, in this case the Negro, are innately inferior and will always remain so. Others acknowledge that there may be some differences between groups, but they hold that these differences do not exist because of any inherent racial inferiority or superiority. The obvious clash between these two lines of thought creates the present crisis.

How should Christian people think and act in facing the race problem? What part should churches play in providing some solution to the problem? The answers to these questions are not easy, but they must be sought.

Development of the Race Problem

To think and act intelligently, the Christian must gain historical perspective. He should understand the conditions under which the Negro came to this country. He should know what forces helped to mold the life and character of the Negro. Above all else, the Christian should seek to benefit from this historical perspective. Wherever injustice has been incurred, he should be ready to strive for justice.

Beginning of slavery in the colonies.—Negroes did not choose to be Americans. They were taken by force from the land which they called home. Contrary to their wishes they were brought to a new and strange land. Furthermore, they were treated as a mere commodity on the market; they were sold to the colonists as slaves. "According to John Smith's *Generall Historie of Virginia,* there arrived in Jamestown in 1619 'a Dutch man of warre [sic], that sold us twenty negars.' " [1] This took place only twelve years after the first prominent British settlement in the colonies, and it was before the landing of the Pilgrim Fathers in Plymouth in 1620.

It is difficult to realize how cruelly the Negro was treated as he was brought to this land. "Negroes were carried in the holds of those sailing vessels in much the same manner as livestock is hauled in trucks today." [2] The Negroes must have wondered what the future held for them as they made their way across the Atlantic.

In speaking of the ship which brought the twenty Negroes to Virginia in 1619, Soper says that "from that beginning the importation of Negroes continued for nearly two centuries." He makes a valid observation when he says that the problem which is created by the presence of the Negro today is not one of his own devising. "It is one for which the white men are solely responsible, and which had its beginnings very early in our history."

---

[1] Edmund Davison Soper, *Racism a World Issue* (New York: Abingdon-Cokesbury Press, 1947), p. 220.

[2] Frank O. Bregnard, *I Understand the South* (New York: Vantage Press, 1956), p. 11.

Growth of slavery.—Very little stood in the way of the growth of slavery. Selfish men learned rapidly how to exploit slave labor. As the agriculture of the colonies developed, the importation of slaves grew proportionately. The great development in tobacco growing speeded up importation and by 1740 about 140,000 Negro slaves had been imported into the colonies.

In the latter half of the eighteenth century the fear of insurrection led some of the colonial legislatures to seek some restriction of the slaves. The spirit of freedom at the time of the Revolution combined with the overproduction of tobacco to discourage slavery, but the attitude toward the Negro was the same. Thomas Jefferson sought to write a clause into the Declaration of Independence against slave importation, but it was rejected.

The institution of slavery was to gain further impetus. The invention of the cotton gin in 1793 opened a new field for the profitable use of slave labor. Although most of the states had stopped slave importation, South Carolina reopened her ports in 1803. In 1808, Congress enacted a law prohibiting further importation of slaves. This law was not rigidly enforced, and by the time of the War Between the States there were about four million slaves in the United States.

Civil War days.—The matter of slavery brought conflict between the North and the South. This conflict finally took the form of warfare. Ministers were found on both sides of the question. In the North the majority of the preachers were condemning slavery as being contrary to the Bible and its teachings. The story was quite different in the South. Many of the "ministers of the gospel were proving to their own satisfaction that slavery was encouraged in the Bible and that it was conformable to Christian tradition." [3] Opposition to slavery on moral grounds gained little hearing in the South.

The Civil War came to an end, and the Negro at least gained a point in principle. The Emancipation Proclamation was promulgated by Abraham Lincoln January 1, 1863, and a new era in the life of the Negroes in America was begun. This proclamation applied only in the states which had revolted. Slavery as a whole ceased December 18, 1865, when the Thirteenth Amendment to the Constitution became part of the basic law of the United States.

---

[3] Soper, *op. cit.*, pp. 221–22.

Reconstruction days.—In some ways the reconstruction days after the Civil War were days of new freedom and new ventures for the Negro. Although he was still hated by many, he was a free man.

The legislation of the Congress during reconstruction, which was "designed to elevate the freedman and nullify the black codes, included the Fourteenth and Fifteenth Amendments, and the civil rights acts of 1866, 1870, and 1875." [4] Among the provisions of the Fourteenth Amendment was the stipulation that all who were born or naturalized in the United States were citizens, and they were not to be deprived of life, liberty, or property without due process of law. The Fifteenth Amendment assured the right of all citizens to vote, regardless of race, color, or previous condition of servitude. The legislation of the reconstruction era favored the Negro.

"In 1883 the Supreme Court declared the Civil Rights Bill of 1875 unconstitutional in so far as it referred to acts of social discrimination by individuals." [5] This left the way open for the "Jim Crow" legislation in the South. However, the South had to get around the constitutional provision that Negroes were to enjoy full citizenship. The legal term for this craft in the social field is "separate-but-equal." "Jim Crow" laws did not come into being until about the turn of the century. It is probable that most southerners consider them to have always existed.

The Supreme Court.—Since it is the duty of the Supreme Court to uphold justice, it is helpful to observe the trends of this body. The attitude before the Civil War may be seen in the Dred Scott decision of 1857. It showed that the Negro was considered so far inferior that he had no rights which the white man was bound to respect. After the Civil War, the Court still was not favorable to the Negro. The length to which the Court went is seen when it is observed that it "even forbade the states to enforce their own laws against discrimination in traveling; a Louisiana law had prohibited such discriminations." [6]

An important case which came before the Supreme Court was the *Plessy* v. *Ferguson* case of 1896. The essence of the Court's decision was that it was all right to segregate, but the state must afford to each

---

[4] Herbert Hill and Jack Greenberg, *Citizen's Guide to Desegregation* (Boston: The Beacon Press, 1955), p. 7.

[5] Arnold Rose, *The Negro in America* (New York: Harper & Bros., 1944), p. 191.

[6] Hill and Greenberg, *op. cit.*, p. 9.

of its citizens equal rights before the law and also equal opportunities for improvement and progress. This case takes on primary importance when it is noted that "all legal segregation since 1896 has rested on the separate-but-equal doctrine of the case of *Plessy* v. *Ferguson*." [7]

In the 1930s the attitude of the Court seemed to turn some toward favoring the rights of Negroes. The next two decades saw a slow but definite trend toward consideration of the rights of the Negro. The culmination of this interest came on May 17, 1954, when the Supreme Court declared the separate-but-equal doctrine to be unconstitutional. In effect, this was ordering that all such discrimination with respect to public facilities should cease. Realizing that this would be a tremendous stride for the American people, the Court did not demand immediate implementation. It was a year later, May 31, 1955, that the Court ruled that a "prompt and reasonable start toward full compliance" would have to be made. Thus, in theory at least, the Negro has been granted his rights and privileges and freedom. Just how complete this victory is for the Negro remains to be observed.

Contemporary Conditions

Having seen the general historical development of the race problem in the United States, attention can now be turned to contemporary conditions. This will involve the general results that have come from the historical setting.

Lack of communication between races.—There is today in the South less real communication between Negroes and whites than ever before in the nation's history. This would be denied by many white southerners, for they feel that they know and understand the Negro quite well. They feel that the southern Negro is really satisfied.

At least some Negroes are aware of the lack of communication and understanding. They blame the white man for failing to understand them. They are especially resentful of the attitude of some southerners who feel that the Negro of slavery days was quite happy. "Today Negroes, young and old, resent the assertion that they were contented as slaves." [8] The southern white man does not seem to know and understand the Negro today. Real communication between the races is greatly needed.

---

[7] *Ibid.*

[8] Robert R. Moton, *What the Negro Thinks* (New York: Doubleday, Doran & Co., 1929), p. 9.

Abuses of the Negro.—The abuses heaped on the Negro have run the gamut of violent acts. The Emancipation Proclamation of 1863, in some instances, did little except incite violence. For even "in 1868 one hundred and twenty black bodies were found in Bossier Parish, Louisiana, following a 'nigger hunt.' " And the violence has continued through the years.

The burning of Henry Lowry in Arkansas proceeded by inches. Leaves soaked in gasoline were heaped about in small bundles so that torture would be dragged out. Ralph Roddy, a reporter, described the entire orgy in the Memphis *Press* of January 27, 1921. He was able to cover the story because plans for the lynching had been made well in advance and the newspapers notified to be ready to issue extras. When Henry Smith was burned at the stake in Texas, excursion trains were run for the event and many women and children were in the throng that gloated over the sufferings of the victim.[9]

Most violence toward Negroes has been dispelled, but not all abuse is of this nature. One of the most inconsistent and unforgivable abuses is the refusal of the white man to acknowledge the human dignity of the Negro woman. Seemingly, with little conscience, the white man has taken advantage of her. Yet emotions rise in hatred, and are expressed sometimes in murder, if a Negro man even so much as looks upon a white woman. One Negro writer says that "there may be an element of perverted conscience in the white man's violent anxiety to protect female purity. His own crimes against colored women may have given him an unholy sensitiveness." [10]

There are many abuses of an important but nonviolent nature. Time and time again the Negro is inconvenienced or deprived because of abusive treatment. Embree aptly illustrates this point. "A brilliant Negro scholar recently spent weeks reading the volumes he needed in his historical research in the men's washroom of a 'public' library because he could not take the books out with him and was not allowed to use them in the reading room." To consider all of the abuses directed toward the Negro would fill a very large volume.

A basic problem—prejudice.—It is appalling to witness the prejudice which many southerners hold against the Negro. Parents are

---

[9] Edwin R. Embree, *Brown Americans* (New York: The Viking Press, 1943), p. 169.
[10] *Ibid.*, p. 170.

responsible, to a great extent, for passing on much of their prejudice to their children. "It is when frightened parents erect prohibitions that the seeds of prejudice are planted. These in most cases are planted and grow luxuriously." [11]

When white children in urban and rural sections of Georgia and in urban areas of Tennessee were compared with children attending an all-white school in New York City, their basic attitudes toward the Negro were found to be the same. Students of the problem now generally accept the view that children's attitudes toward Negroes are determined chiefly "not by contact with Negroes but by contacts with the prevailing attitudes toward Negroes." It is not the Negro child, but the *idea* of the Negro child, that influences children. [12]

Wherever prejudice gets its start, it is fully exhibited by adults. Just how ridiculous it causes some adults to act is seen in the following account:

Representative Hendricks of Florida, in supporting the attack of the Dies Committee on William Pickens, a Negro treasury employee, as recently as 1943 apologized to the House for his mistake in saying "Mr. Pickens." "I didn't know the man was black," said Hendricks. "Any man from the South doesn't call a colored man 'Mr.'" Some years ago a witness who persisted, after a warning, in referring to a Negro defendant as Mr. Scott was fined for contempt of court. A Negro who asked for a can of Prince Albert tobacco was shown the picture of the white Prince Albert on the can and forced to call for "Mr. Prince Albert" before he could get the tobacco. [13]

It is no wonder that the Negro sometimes questions the intelligence of the white man. Many men seem not to realize that their ways and thoughts are directed by prejudice rather than by well-founded facts.

Limited rights of Negroes.—The rights of Negroes which are limited by the attitudes of white men are far too many to enumerate, but some of them should be noted.

Probably the most important limitation has been that imposed upon the Negro's right to vote. This has been important, for to have fully the

---

[11] Georgia Harkness, *Christian Ethics* (New York: Abingdon Press, 1957), pp. 166–67.

[12] Kenneth B. Clark, *Prejudice and Your Child* (Boston: The Beacon Press, 1955), p. 25.

[13] Embree, *op. cit.,* p. 164.

right to vote would be for the Negro to possess the power in many instances to overcome other limitations of rights. Various means have been used to keep the Negro from voting. In some instances tests of literacy have been established. To keep from depriving white men of their vote, some states created what was called the "Grandfather's Clause." This simply stated that "a person might be excused from being able to read or knowing the Constitution if he, his father, or grandfather had voted before 1867." [14]

There is an economic factor in the problem of voting limitation. The poll tax is required in several states as a prerequisite to voting. It is commonly acknowledged that the original purpose of this tax was to deprive the Negro of his right to vote. It is argued by some that this tax deprives some whites of voting also, and this is true. However, the fact remains that it was intended to limit the Negro's rights, and the end result is just that. As long as the Negro does not have complete freedom to carry out his right of voting, other limitations upon his rights will continue to exist.

So-called Negro inferiority.—Many southern white men are convinced that the Negro is innately inferior. Some intelligence tests were given to inductees, both Negro and white, during World War I. The results of these tests were not too complimentary to the South.

Median Scores on A.E.F. Intelligence Tests [15]

Southern Whites:	
Mississippi	41.25
Kentucky	41.50
Arkansas	41.55
Northern Negroes:	
New York	45.02
Illinois	47.35
Ohio	49.50

These statistics seem to indicate that the Negro's ability does not depend on his racial characteristics but on his environment and opportunity to improve.

No one will argue against the fact that many Negroes today are actually inferior in their abilities, but it *must* be realized that this is not an inherent inferiority. Their inferiority is not a product of God's

---

[14] Bregnard, *op. cit.*, p. 35.
[15] T. B. Maston, *Of One*, p. 69.

hand; it is a product of American society. If inferiority is thus produced, the laws of the society need to be re-examined.

Christian Reaction to the Racial Situation

What are the churches doing with the race problem? How do Christians feel about the Negro? Is there any real concern on the part of Christianity? These are pertinent questions.

The churches and pronouncements.—Pronouncements have been forthcoming from Christian groups in the United States. Generally, the churches, by separate action and in their councils, have in their official statements repudiated segregation in principle. However, there is general agreement that pronouncements have certain limitations. "Valuable as they are as standard-setters, pronouncements have the inherent limitation in that they are made, as a rule, not by the rank and file, but by a few persons whom special circumstances have subjected to liberalizing influences." [16] In many instances they represent a minority opinion, thus detracting from their usefulness and validity.

It should not be construed that no pronouncements should be made. They can become very useful. "Some of the statements . . . represent much serious thought and careful consideration on the part of the bodies responsible for them. Others have less intrinsic authority or significance but are noteworthy because they have at least the weight of official declarations and may be used in educational work among the communions originating them." [17]

Loescher also quotes J. H. Oldham as suggesting another use for pronouncements. "Authoritative statements of this kind may often be a strength and support to individual ministers in interpreting the ethical implications of the gospel in face of criticism and opposition."

T. B. Maston praises both the statement made at the St. Louis meeting of the Southern Baptist Convention in 1947 and the approval of the Supreme Court decision by the 1954 convention. He adds, however, that "a pronouncement is one thing and its practical application in the local church, community, and in the Baptist fellowship in general is quite another thing." [18]

---

[16] Frank S. Loescher, *The Protestant Church and the Negro* (New York: Association Press, 1948), p. 48.

[17] *Ibid.*

[18] *Integration* (Nashville: Christian Life Commission of the Southern Baptist Convention, 1956), p. 14.

The churches and their practices.—Since it has been suggested that there might be a difference between the official pronouncements of Christian bodies and their actual practice, it may be well to make a comparison.

In reality, segregation is the rule. While some Christian bodies in their pronouncements speak favorably of desegregation, in practice they are quite segregated. One writer states that "never is our city more segregated than on Sunday morning at eleven." [19] The writer substantiates this conclusion with the statement that in 1954, of fifty-six million American Protestants, less than half of one per cent of Negroes worshiped on a nonsegregated basis. The restrictions of segregation are imposed only on the Negro. "Negroes are not admitted to white churches in the South, but if a strange white man enters a Negro church the visit is received as a great honor." [20] It is clear that the rules of segregation are intended for the so-called protection of whites and are directed against the Negroes.

The pronouncements of churches and Christian bodies indicate that men are equal. Unfortunately, many southerners, even those in the churches, adhere to the doctrine of white supremacy. Earl Conrad went to Alabama to make a special study of the situation there. His general attitude was that of sympathy with the Negro. He pointed out that he saw many churches in the area, and he wondered if there was not some help coming from these churches. A Negro leader told him that the churches were not much different from the state in their attitudes. The churches were as segregated as the residential areas. And then he summed it up by saying, "Christ preaches white supremacy down here, you know." [21]

The sociologists speak of a cultural lag. Christian leaders might well speak of a spiritual lag. In searching through writings to see what men have had to say about the race problem, it is interesting but appalling to find that those who are speaking most clearly and courageously are those representing secular fields. There is a rather obvious silence among Christian leaders. Why should this be? Does God no longer call prophets?

---

[19] Walter White, *How Far the Promised Land?* (New York: Harper & Bros., 1955), p. 194.

[20] Rose, *op. cit.,* p. 190.

[21] Earl Conrad, *Jim Crow America* (New York: Duell, Sloan & Pearce, 1947), p. 10.

The principles of the Bible speak very clearly to the Christian mind. The spirit of God deeply impresses the Christian conscience to bring about a spirit of justice. Many Christians have long known what is right. "But we white Christians waited too long. The Supreme Court had to tell us. Christ forgive us for this neglect! Surely, the least we can do is to sit down with our Negro brothers and try now to be reconciled with them." [22]

The Great Obstacle—Intermarriage

There are many facets to the race problem. There are many difficulties which are complex. There are many objections which are raised. There is, however, no objection or problem which is raised more often than that of intermarriage. It looms as such a great problem that it is worthy of separate consideration.

Southern white attitudes.—"The Southern man on the street responds to any plea for social equality: 'Would you like to have your daughter marry a Negro?' " [23] Apart from this problem, it is possible that the southern white man might be led to accord justice and decent treatment to the Negro. But inevitably "when decent treatment of the Negroes is urged, a certain class of people hurry to raise the scarecrow of social mingling and intermarriage." [24]

An individual with any Negro blood is considered to be Negro. Consequently, illicit relations between white men and colored women affect only the Negro race. It is obvious that if the illicit relation occurs between a Negro man and a white woman, the consequences of any offspring would be quite different. The child would be considered Negro, and the white woman would be degraded. Therefore, the southern white man feels it is his responsibility to use every means possible to protect the white woman. To accomplish this, legal means are used.

The important thing to notice concerning the southern attitude on intermarriage is the inconsistency of beliefs and practice. With great vehemence the southern white man has denounced any social contact with the Negro. At the apex of his denunciations is that of intermarriage. Many a southern white man would be willing to give his

---

[22] R. Lofton Hudson, "What Would Jesus Have Us Do?" *Christian Faith in Action,* comp., Foy Valentine (Nashville: Broadman Press, 1956), p. 92.
[23] Rose, *op. cit.,* p. 195.
[24] Embree, *op. cit.,* p. 181.

own life to protect these standards; yet his moral standards betray him. "Almost all of race mixture in America has come not at the Negro's wish but by the acts of those very white men who talked loudest of 'race purity.' " [25]

The southern white man has stood firmly against social contact with the Negroes and intermarriage, but "by the time of the Civil War there were few Negroes left in the country of 'purely African blood.' The mulatto was bred in the South by the white man from helpless slave women." [26] The inconsistency between belief and practice seems clear.

The Negro's viewpoint.—For a long time it did not matter at all what the Negro thought. The Negro slave could think as long as he did not think out loud. The days of slavery came to an end, but the days of discrimination were far from being at an end. Almost a century later, the Negro still does not have his full rights.

Some changes have taken place. The Negro of slavery days was ignorant and uneducated; today he is gaining some educational opportunities. The Negro of slavery days had not freedom to speak; today he is beginning to speak what is on his mind. With greater freedom to speak, and with a greater ability to speak, his demands are becoming stronger.

It should be noted that if the Negro demands the *right* of intermarriage, it does not necessarily mean that he wants intermarriage. The Negro is convinced that the present system is unfair. Booker T. Washington once asked a piercing question: "If your segregation wall be high enough to keep the black man in, will it be high enough to keep the white man out?"

The Negro wonders why the southern white man is so concerned to have a ban on intermarriage *if,* as it is claimed, there is no attraction between the two races. "In using the danger of intermarriage as a defense for the whole caste system, it is assumed both that Negro men have a strong desire for 'intermarriage' and that white women would be open to proposals from Negro men *if* they were not guarded from even meeting them on an equal plane." [27] Furthermore, the Negro finds it very difficult to understand why such intermarriage should draw criticism and blame only on the Negro's side. Along this line,

[25] *Ibid.*
[26] *Ibid.*
[27] Rose, *op. cit.,* p. 194.

T. B. Maston says, "Every such marriage involves a white person as well as a Negro. Why put all the blame on the Negro?" The only answer that the Negro finds is that the white man has placed a stamp of inferiority on him.

Christian attitude on intermarriage.—The matter of intermarriage is a complex and difficult one. It involves emotions, prejudice, and social implications which cannot be ignored. There is no simple answer, but there must be an attitude which is Christian in its spirit. "The question of social equality and intermarriage tend to disturb most Southern whites, but there is a prior and more important question for Christians which is the most disturbing of all—what is the Christian thing to do?" [28]

The Christian must find dissatisfaction in the present state of affairs. What Christian can stand idly by in satisfaction as white men deplore social equality and at the same time invade the privacy and dignity of Negro women through illicit relations with them? One has said, "Either legitimate amalgamation should be allowed or illegitimate should cease. And the burden of responsibility in the matter is not on the Negro. It is on the white." [29] It should be obvious that the Christian would demand that illicit relations should cease.

Not only should the Christian be dissatisfied with conditions as they are, he can find grounds for granting the *right* of intermarriage. Harkness says "that there is no law of God against such intermarriage, and there ought to be none of the state." One Christian group has declared:

> While it can find in the Bible no clear justification or condemnation of intermarriage, but only a discussion of the duties of the faithful in marriage with partners of other religions, it cannot approve any law against racial or ethnic intermarriage, for Christian marriage involves primarily a union of two individuals before God which goes beyond the jurisdiction of the state or of culture.[30]

If Negroes are accepted as equals, and if they are given their full rights, it follows that the privilege of intermarriage ought to be

---

[28] Maston, *Of One*, p. 94.

[29] Robert B. Speer, *Of One Blood* (New York: Council of Women for Home Missions and Missionary Education Movement of the United States and Canada, 1924), p. 188.

[30] Harkness, *op. cit.*, p. 171.

allowed. It has been previously stated that generally the Negroes do not want intermarriage, but in facing reality it must be acknowledged that there would be some exceptions. Embree says that "making democracy real for Negroes might raise the number of marriages, but it would certainly slow down the promiscuous mingling that now goes on, a process much more harmful to a stabilized society than marriage between equals could possibly be." [31] If he means that a law is going to change men's minds about promiscuity, the statement is to be doubted; but if he means that such a law might lift a relationship from promiscuity to the realm of legitimate marriage, he has a point. Some intermarriages have produced effective, happy Christian homes; others have not. Hasty generalizations must be avoided, here as elsewhere.

Although in principle, the Christian can grant the right to intermarriage, there is more to be said on the matter. While the principle of freedom and equality is maintained, the virtues of wisdom and common sense must be employed. There might be many good reasons to disapprove a marriage between Negro and white. As in any contemplated marriage, the backgrounds, abilities, likes, and dislikes of a couple must be considered; and the couple who would consider intermarriage must face the society in which they would live. Under contemporary circumstances, they would not be well received by either whites or Negroes. The effect of these circumstances on their children certainly should be considered.

While the Christian attitude may grant the *right* of intermarriage, the Christain may also advisedly feel that intermarriage is not the answer to the problems which exist today. As one has said, "Miscegenation ought not to be encouraged. Not because any biological inferiority results from a mixing of racial stocks, but because in the present state of society tensions are more often increased than abated by it. Intermarriage is on the whole a step away from a solution of the race problem rather than toward it." [32]

A Christian Perspective for Today

Being aware of the race problem, the Christian must seek to gain perspective. He must view the whole world and recognize its needs.

[31] *Op. cit.,* p. 182.
[32] Harkness, *op. cit.,* p. 170.

He must look to God whom he worships and seek to understand him better. Through introspection, the Christian must gain a better knowledge of himself and his attitudes and responsibilities. He must make every effort to better understand the Negro and his problems.

Few men are ready or willing to act in behalf of any cause until they see a need for action. The cause of better race relations is no exception. The compelling need must be recognized.

It should be realized that national prestige is at stake. From many distant points in the world there comes the criticism that the United States is not really the land of freedom and equality which it claims to be. To substantiate these accusations, the accusers point to the treatment of the Negro. Harkness points out also that communism can make no claim to complete racial equality, because the Jews have been discriminated against in Russia and elsewhere. Nevertheless, "it is certain that our racial inequalities, though exaggerated, are a chief weapon in the psychological war against us."

As the Christian views the total world situation, he must realize that the cause of foreign missions inevitably suffers because of racial discrimination in the United States. The spread of the gospel at home and abroad is greatly handicapped when its representatives are not examples of its teachings in their own lives. M. Theron Rankin, a missionary to China and later executive secretary of the Southern Baptist Foreign Mission Board, is quoted as saying, "More and more the sincerity of our interest in the colored peoples within their native lands will be judged by our treatment of the peoples of those lands who live in our country." As the Christian seeks to gain perspective by viewing the whole world, he begins to realize that the very cause of Christ is involved in the problem.

No view of the world is complete unless the situation at home is considered. Even if foreign prestige and foreign missions were not at stake, the situation at home is enough in itself to compel the Christian to give attention to the race problem.

The psychology which is involved in discrimination is disheartening to the Negro. Any sign which tells him to sit at the rear of the bus or avoid quenching his thirst at a fountain is saying in essence, "You are an inferior being." This attitude of discrimination is a vicious circle. Many southerners feel that the Negro masses are actually inferior and that this gives reason for discrimination against them. At the same time, discrimination makes it difficult for the Negro to improve himself. Discrimination assures the actual inferiority of many Negroes, and many whites prefer that they remain so.

Can the Christian today overlook his need for a new perspective?

The Christian's Relation to the Problem

It may be possible for the Christian to see the compelling needs with respect to the race problem and still do nothing about it. In this case, he has failed to realize his relation to the task.

The better the Christian understands the nature of God, the better he will understand his own relation to the racial problem. God is a universal God. He is a God of justice, mercy, and love. God cannot be a racial nor a national God. He cannot be a "class" God. He must be a God for all people. How unfortunate it is when God is blamed for the discrimination of today. God made the races, for he made all men, and it might be that he would be satisfied if they chose to maintain their racial characteristics. However, God will never be satisfied with the present attitude which considers one race innately *inferior* and the other innately *superior*.

What is needed today is a theology which is expressed in action. Vague generalities about the fatherhood of God and the brotherhood of man are often spoken but do not cut down through our crust of convention to where the race problem is. When men know God in his true nature of love and compassion, they will be compelled to share his love with all men.

As the Christian comes to understand better the nature of God, he should also come to understand better the function of the church with which he is affiliated. It is the church's business to be in the vanguard of the moral forces of society, including the race problem.

The race problem today is primarily in the hands of the politicians. To a certain degree, this is as it should be; this is especially true as the politicians are guided by Christian principles. The mistake is made when the church assumes a hands-off policy and leaves such problems entirely to the judgment of the politicians. In this instance the church feels no responsibility at all.

Furthermore, if a thing be right, what better place could there be to demonstrate the truth than in the church? If the Christian viewpoint is that segregation is discriminatory in nature and wrong in the eyes of God, then the church is the logical place for segregation to be abolished. "The church is not only following the community patterns of segregation; . . . [it] is lagging behind the local customs. Its practices actually help to perpetuate the system of segregation." [33] If the Christian is to be properly related to the racial problem through his church then some changes must be made.

Negro attitudes and demands must be understood.—The Negro has often been wrongly accused concerning his attitudes. If the white man were accorded the same treatment as the Negroes, he would "rise up in arms." This the Negro has done at times but these times have been very few. Moton says that "in his forgiving moods the Negro actually pities the condition of the man who cannot, and who dare not even, recognize skill and talent, honour and virtue, strength and goodness simply because it wears a black skin." [34] Even when Negroes have been obviously and openly mistreated, they have often followed the admirable path of passive resistance. Martin Luther King, Jr. voiced the sentiment of the Negro attitude in Montgomery, Alabama, when he said, "If we are arrested every day, if we are exploited every day, if we are trampled over every day, don't ever let anyone pull you so low as to hate them. We must use the weapon of love. We must have compassion and understanding for those who hate us. We must realize so many people are taught to hate us that they are not totally responsible for their hate. But we stand in life at midnight; we are always on the threshold of a new dawn."

Furthermore, the attitude of the Negroes is not that of being entirely right while others are all wrong. One Negro has said that "there is no use pretending that Negroes are better than they are. Many are shiftless and undependable, just like persons in other groups." If white Christians would take the same objective point of view, there would be much common ground upon which Negro and white might walk together.

One writer has said that "happily our problem is half solved by the attitude of the Negro race." [35] To say that the race problem is half solved may be too optimistic, but proper attitudes on the part of the Negroes should be noticed. When such attitudes are apparent, there should be a complementary response from the whites.

Negroes are making new demands. Would the Christian deny the

[33] Loescher, *op. cit.*, p. 106.

[34] *Op. cit.*, p. 220.

[35] Robert E. Smith, *Christianity and the Race Problem* (New York: Fleming H. Revell & Co., 1922), p. 116.

Negro the right to make these demands? What is the Negro demanding today? It is the abolishment of segregation—forced separation, and unless he is lower than a human being, the Negro has a right to make this demand. He is not demanding that everything be integrated. Desegregation is a better word to express his wishes. This allows separation of races, but it would be voluntary rather than forced. Despite the propaganda in the newspapers, generally the southern Negro does not particularly *want* his children to go to integrated schools. And, with but few exceptions, the Negro is far better satisfied to go to his own church than he would be to go to an integrated one. Although this observation may be true, it remains for white Christians to make it possible for Negroes to make a free and voluntary choice.

As demands are made, the Christian must realize that the Negro, as all men, is made in the image of God. Therefore, he has every right to make his demands.

Methods must be considered.—It is possible for Christians to see the needs involved in the race problem, feel responsible to do something, and yet fail to carry out this responsibility. Thought must be given to ways in which they can carry out their convictions. This may sometimes involve a step-by-step procedure. More often, however, it will involve certain principles which will determine the best methods.

Christians must begin where they are. Some do more harm than good at times, even though their convictions are fine. In seeking to eradicate past wrongs, all that is done must be based on things as they are and not as they are supposed to be. It would be convenient if people were not prejudiced, but they are. Thus a process of education must be utilized. It is true that this method may move rather slowly, but basic social changes which are brought about through carefully prepared and wisely directed educational media will be more enduring in the long run. A group, or a church, must be led, not forced, to believe that a thing is right. Patience must continue to be a Christian virtue.

To say that the Christian must sometimes wait for prejudice to be overcome is not to say that he himself is to lower his standards or to change his convictions. Above all else, he must continue to look to the ideals and principles which he derives from God's Word. It is only as some adhere to the ideals that others will be detracted from their prejudice. It must always be remembered that the task of the churches is to preach and to teach the principles of original Christianity in their purity. The race problem today is greatly magnified by the fact that many Christians have compromised their ideals and have accommodated their views to those whose ideals are sub-Christian. Such a compromise is not the proper Christian procedure.

It has already been suggested that it will be necessary for the Christian to face reality in the present circumstances. On the other hand, it has been indicated that the ideal must be maintained. As these two factors are brought together, the real and the ideal, there is obvious tension. There is need at times for Christians to create some tension in order to make progress. Race equality will not arrive all at once, nor will it arrive at all unless we cease conforming to prevailing attitudes and practices and give the church an opportunity to lead in the shaping of community standards. Sometimes very bold steps need to be taken in order to awaken the Christian conscience. At other times it is necessary to move more slowly. Always the matter of tension should be brought into play in order to move closer to the Christian ideal.

Christians must give some hope for the present. The Negro has exhibited a commendable patience. It is not enough to tell the Negro that some day, maybe in the next generation, things will be better. The Negro today has the right to expect that things will be better in his own lifetime. He may not get all that he wants or deserves, but he should find some improvement.

A liberal white acquaintance and a Negro woman were discussing in my presence the question of whether Negro liberation would come soon or late, and the white woman said: "Personally, I don't think the Negro will be fully delivered from his social condition until there is a complete amalgamation of colored and white. That might take several hundred years." The colored woman looked at the back of her hand, which was brown, and remarked, "You mean I've got to wait until my hand gets white?" [36]

The Negro will not get all that he deserves now, but he should not have to wait forever to receive some new rights and privileges. The Christian perspective will not allow it.

---

[36] Conrad, *op. cit.,* p. 199.

Additional Reading

CROOK, ROGER H. *No South or North.* St. Louis: The Bethany Press, 1959.

GOERNER, CORNELL. "Race Relations: A Factor in World Missions," a tract published by the Christian Life Commission of the Southern Baptist Convention.

HASELDEN, KYLE. *The Racial Problem in Christian Perspective.* New York: Harper & Bros., 1959.

MASTON, T. B. *The Bible and Race.* Nashville: Broadman Press, 1959.

————. *Segregation and Desegregation: A Christian Approach.* New York: The Macmillan Co., 1959.

POPE, LISTON. *The Kingdom Beyond Caste.* New York: Friendship Press, 1957.

ROBINSON, JAMES H. "Race Relations and International Problems," *Missions,* March 1, 1953.

WASSON, ALFRED. "Race and the World Mission of the Church"; "Christianity and Race," *The Perkins School of Theology Journal,* Spring, 1958.

8

Meeting the Challenge of Communism

W. RANDALL LOLLEY

In the year 1927, a Chinese girl was condemned to death for Communist revolutionary activities. To her sorrowing family she said, "Don't weep for me. I'm dying for a cause. What are you continuing to live for?" The essence of the Communist challenge is captured in this statement. Communism poses a challenge, especially to Christianity, simply because Communists consider their cause worth their living and dying. In their "big leap" Communists are calling the world's attention once more to the revolutionary power of a new affection.

Victor Hugo once said, "There is one thing stronger than all the armies in the world and that is an idea whose time has come." Presumably this is true of an evil as well as a good idea. Such a time came for the idea of communism slightly over one hundred years ago. There had been forms of communism through the long centuries of human history. But on March 27, 1844, in the city of Paris, France, Karl Marx met Friedrich Engels, and since that time communism as the world presently knows it has had a theoretical foundation as well as a practical program for conquering the world.

One sentence from Marx reveals the militant nature of his idea: "The philosophers have only interpreted the world, in various ways; the point, however, is to *change* it." [1] From a small and inauspicious beginning communism has made its thrust into history as a restless, ruthless world conquerer.

---

[1] Karl Marx and Friedrich Engels, *Basic Writings on Politics and Philosophy,* ed. Lewis S. Feuer (Garden City: Doubleday & Co., 1959), p. 245.

It should be acknowledged that Communist totalitarianism and democracy are more than mere social, political, or economic systems. They are two diametrically opposed ways of life, with contradicting beliefs and values, based on distinct and opposite concepts of the nature of man. The scope and gravity of the present world crisis can, therefore, be fully grasped only by perceiving it as a conflict between two ways of thought and action, encompassing the totality of organized human life. Such an analysis of the present situation has led some to define communism as "basically *a way of life* rooted in a certain belief about the world, about man and society, and about the movement of history." [2] That belief and way of life stand in irreconcilable opposition to the Christian faith.

Communism is a system involving human beings in relation. In fact, its basic dynamic is the belief that here is a system which will eventually guarantee perfect human relationships. Its goal is an ideal temporal manifestation of "persons in society"—a fellowship of individuals in classless bliss.

The opening words of Marx and Engel's *Communist Manifesto* of 1848 were: "A spectre is haunting Europe—the spectre of Communism." Obviously, from what follows in the *Manifesto,* the main reason for the spectre's haunting Europe was that the system whereby persons found themselves in economic, political, and social relationships was sick unto death.

Communism was stalking the land, awaiting the time when the exigencies of the intolerable situation would explode it and thus allow the advance guard of the proletarians to usher in their own program for "persons in society."

This same *Communist Manifesto* closed with these words: "The proletarians have nothing to lose but their chains. They have a world to win. Working men of all countries, unite!" In this clarion call the working thesis of communism was born. That thesis originally was: "From each according to his ability, to each according to his need." It soon became obvious that this pattern was a bit too optimistic for immediate realization. Therefore, in Stalin's Constitution of 1936, the thesis was revised to read: "From each according to his ability, to each according to his work." This is said to be the temporary situation during the present (socialist) phase of development in the Soviet

---

[2] *The Challenge of Communism* (London: SCM Press, 1952), p. 5.

Union and will revert to the original formula in the final Communist phase.

It is evident that the critical sphere for communism is the social arena of persons in relationship. It is here that the Communists found the ground for beginning, and it is here that they have formulated their program for advance. It is here, likewise, that any effective counter-strategy must come most directly to bear. Therefore, an attempt will be made to define the Communist challenge from a Christian perspective, with special emphasis in the crucial area of human relations, and to formulate some lines of strategy whereby Christians may effectively meet the challenge.

The Communist Challenge Reviewed

The free world today faces the issue of survival as it has never faced it before. *Communist man* confronts *the free man*. Khrushchev, more than any other, has made clear "the complete irreconcilability of these two patterns of man; and in doing so, he has helped us to know where our loyalties and our efforts must lie." [3]

What exactly has contributed to the making of this "Communist man"? The answer is the Communist ideology; i.e., the complex of ideas and pressures which converge upon a person to transform him into a Communist. In the background are the ideas of at least three persons from whom Marx borrowed much of his philosophy. From the complex philosophical system of G. W. F. Hegel, Marx borrowed his method of "scientifically" analyzing history through the dialectical determination of events. Here is the source of his oft-mentioned triad of thesis, antithesis, and synthesis. From Ludwig Feuerbach, Marx grasped the idea that God is man's invention, and that in reality there is nothing beyond nature (matter). From Pierre Joseph Proudhon, Marx seized the concept of history's bearing within itself the inherent germs of progress. If left to the forces at work in the ebb and flow of time, it was thought that history itself would inevitably issue in a better human society. Marx met Proudhon in Paris, admired him, and adopted his view that the philosopher has not only the task of interpreting the world but of altering it.

The blend of ideas which resulted from Marx's eclectic philosophi-

---

[3] Harry A. and Bonaro Overstreet, *The War Called Peace* (New York: W. W. Norton & Co., 1961), p. 7.

cal method has come to be called dialectical materialism (the *diamat*). At its heart this view of the world guarantees that the laws of change, as formulated by the dialectic, are operating pre-eminently in the economic sphere. Therefore, Marx could observe all human history and conclude that the history of the human race is a history of competing economic systems.

An analysis of the Marxian complex of ideas indicates the mental, emotional, and social pressures which contribute to the making of Communist man. He is a man ideologically formed. The *diamat* contains three main theses which constitute the chief ideological thrusts of communism today. First, there is the conviction that progress is inherent in change. Change, in turn, is determined by the inevitabilities of the material universe. Communists perceive themselves to be co-operating with these inevitabilities. Therefore, revolution is the watchword of communism and restlessness is its fundamental nature.

Second, there is the conviction that retreat is an essential part of advance. Communism is often misunderstood at this point. Many times a change in tactics has been interpreted as a change in ideology. The fact is that Communists have had amazing success in adjusting their strategy to the exigencies of any given situation. Consequently, the history of the movement has been marked by an alternating series of retreats and advances. Retreat, however, is always temporary and tactical. Collectivism is held to be inevitable, and the ultimate goal is to achieve it.

Third, there is the conviction that to destroy is to build up. From the Communist perspective man is but matter, molded by laws inherent in matter. There is no such thing as independent reason or an independent will. Individual autonomy simply does not exit. Man is molded by economic forces which are inherent in economic interaction and are parts of the inevitable law of the universe. Liberty does not exist since man can do only what he is compelled to do by economic forces. It is held that only Communists have been conditioned to discover the truth in human developments. All others are either limited, cannot discover the truth, and must be led or they are economically determined not to accept the truth and must be destroyed. The destruction of the individual who refuses to conform to the group is considered a step forward. The group has total control over the individual. Heresies and deviations are diseases in the social body and must be destroyed. A healthy society requires that all its members conform completely to the type required by the society itself.[4]

For Christians, man is created in the image of God; for Communists, he is formed in the image of the Party. Communism possesses completely. It monopolizes all the means of forming a man. Lenin said that his Bolsheviks must "devote to the revolution not only their spare evenings, but the whole of their lives." [5] According to Marxist-Leninist thought, all political, economic, and intellectual life must be regulated by the "proletariat's advance guard," i.e., the Party, because the people and large parts of the proletariat are unable to comprehend the new order. The masses must be guided in a strictly regimented fashion toward participation in the new order.

Communism evidently has the complete propaganda apparatus required to control a man's mind. It extends from kindergarten to university and includes all mass media, i.e., newspapers, movies, radio, and television. In the most cunning ways the ideology is woven in with modern psychological techniques of forming mind and soul. It is able to neutralize and destroy in the most telling way all influences contrary to its goals. The man which the method creates is a human minus all that is distinctly human—a man without spontaneity or freedom of thought, a man completely "part and parcel" of the system. This collective being that has no heart, no feeling, or conscience is a perfect robot of the socialist state.

The constant Communist clamor for a new model of man is based upon the assumption that man is simply a material object in a purely material universe. This being true, man—like cars, refrigerators, or alarm clocks—can be improved and remodeled according to the Party design. The desired product is a person who is standardized and, therefore, totally predictable. That which is standardized and predictable is likewise easily controlled. Thus, Communist man can be relied upon to think what the Party wants thought and to desire what the Party wants him to desire. His is the spirit of collectivism. He feels no need for privacy. He will become thoroughly accustomed to group action and reaction.

---

[4] For a popular discussion of the Communist ideology see the work of Massimo Salvadori, *The Rise of Modern Communism* (New York: Henry Holt & Co., 1952), pp. 91–108.

[5] V. I. Lenin, *Selected Works* (New York: International Publishers, 1943), II, 139.

Moreover, Communist man will feel no desire for a mind of his own. He does not need it. His needs do not require it. He is far removed from being the solitary thinker. Both Marx and Lenin regarded ideas as weapons and minds as targets. In the realm of thought both were military strategists.

Furthermore, the Communist man finds his own culture entirely sufficient. He may venture outside the Iron or Bamboo Curtain in his thoughts, but his curiosity about the world stays within approved limits. He may harbor an intellectual underground, but there is little chance that such thoughts will ever reach the surface and explode his ideological edifice.

Communism's "manufactured" man views the world from a special vantage point. His Marxist-Leninist world view is in reality a strategic view of the world. He sees this planet as a maneuvering place, where the Communist camp must take every advantage to impose its control. For him it is axiomatic that the non-Communist camp is incurably divided and, therefore, vulnerable to Communist attack. For this reason, his relentless campaign *to divide and conquer* must always be in process, by myriad expedient means, in myriad places.

Communist man's view of the world as a maneuvering place determines his opinion of the nature of all contacts between the irreconcilable camps. Such contacts must be controlled from the Communist side. His design in all contacts is summed up in the attitude "penetration without being penetrated." Therefore, the Iron and Bamboo Curtains are no mere manifestations of fear. They are real barriers—borders of the terrain ruled by Communist man. The Marxian man perceives it to be his humane duty to penetrate the non-Communist camp in order to liberate the exploited classes without allowing his own orbit to be penetrated.

Again, Communist man is a resolute and unqualified atheist. His "morals" stem from his complete disregard for any dynamic that religion, in the usual sense, can afford. Yet, he is tolerant of religion when tolerance promotes his cause. Fundamentally, however, he is committed to the proposition that religion and the science of Marxism-Leninism are thoroughly irreconcilable. He must never have that special independence which comes from the inner peace of being at home in the universe—even the material universe of a material man. Communist man, although inevitably destined to inherit the earth, must ever be possessed by an internal unrest which compels him to accept no status quo as ultimately satisfactory. His universe and his destiny are formed in the mold of Marxist materialism untainted by religion.

From the Communist perspective, religion is economically derived. Its taproot is perceived to be a sense of economic insecurity and consequent dependence upon the propertied class. Once this taproot is severed, religion will inevitably die. Marx thought that religion had the same effect as opium on people. By this he meant that religion either lulled the masses into a state of insensitivity to exploitation by the capitalists, or that religion was a pipe dream to exploiter and exploited alike, causing man to seek purpose and comfort in mere illusion.

At this point it is well to mention that communism has been called both "a Western heresy" and "a Christian heresy." It was created in the West on ground prepared by Christianity and was originally designed to promote the proletarian revolution in the capitalistic West rather than in the feudalistic East. John C. Bennett has pointed out that "there is . . . in communism a deposit of Christian influence of great importance; . . . communism could only have developed on soil prepared by Christianity." [6] T. B. Maston has observed that "the lack of vitality and virility in many Christian groups has tended to create a spiritual vacuum at the heart of many nations." [7] Communism, with its sense of purpose and its dynamic program, has been quite successful at moving into that vacuum. In this respect at least the spread of communism constitutes an indictment against the Christian churches.

A careful examination of both the theory and the practice of modern communism reveals just how it is a Western heresy. In theory Marx declared that "dictatorship of the proletariat" was the necessary antithesis of capitalism. By the process of the dialectic he envisaged a time when the synthesis would triumph, resulting in the "classless society." It is remarkable that Marx could have supposed himself capable of determining the precise course that the dialectic would take in the process of unfolding itself. Many diverse elements, which no one person can foresee, can enter to change the final outcome. Such a fact strongly suggests that Marx was expressing an ideological hope rather than a genuine scientific prediction. Moreover, Marx had no genuine

---

[6] *Christianity and Communism Today* (New York: Association Press, 1960), p. 77.

[7] *Christianity and World Issues* (New York: The Macmillan Co., 1957), p. 159.

basis for his assertion that the synthesis would inevitably be the so-called classless society.

In Hegel's use of the dialectic, the synthesis is not something entirely new, emerging for the first time out of the conflict; rather, it could be likened to the phoenix rising from its ashes following the conflagration. The synthesis is simply the reassertion of the original thesis, purged of the original objectionable elements which precipitated the antithesis, and amended by the better elements of the antithesis which it has absorbed. It is difficult to see exactly how the "classless society" is related to the capitalism of which it should theoretically be the reassertion.

In practice the Russian brand of "dictatorship of the proletariat" is not an antithesis of capitalism, for Russia has never known the capitalism of the West. It would be more accurate to say that it is a reaction to the Russian form of feudalism, just as capitalism seems to have been the reaction to feudalism in the West. As a consequence, any future synthesis of modern communism cannot have as its end result the destruction of the worst elements in capitalism. Rather, it must content itself with being, at best, an improvement over the wretched social conditions existing in Russia under the imperialistic and feudalistic czars.

In the West, on the other hand, an entirely different situation has prevailed. The old-time capitalism of the nineteenth and early twentieth centuries was recognized as a gross social evil. Consequently, there followed a social revolution (how much because of Marx's criticism?), expressed clearly at least in one form by the modern labor movement. This social revolution has so transformed the economic thought patterns and social structure of Western capitalism that today the older form of capitalism, which deservedly brought upon itself the reaction of the peoples of the world, no longer exists. In its place a self-corrected form of free enterprise, which still bears the essential features of capitalism, void of much of its social injustices, has arisen. Here is, indeed, an illustration of the reassertion of the original thesis in an adjusted form of synthesis, and it took place as a natural consequence of the historical process, without resorting to any predetermined ideology as to how history *must* unfold itself. Here likewise is the basis for the claim that communism is "a Western heresy."

Another prime feature of the Communist man is his distaste for private property. He is opposed to any and all forms of free enterprise as a basis of economic life. Personal responsibilities and private properties are for him burdensome vestiges of capitalism. The tools of the state and the collectivistic society afford him a certain solicitude completely beyond the ability of most in the West to understand.

In spite of the fact that communism's manufactured man may speak of democracy as a feature of his political order, he really does not think in terms of democracy as the West knows it. Utilizing all the methods of mind-making available through modern science, the Communists make their citizens feel that they are enjoying democracy while they are actually being denied the basic experiences through which genuine democratic habits are formed. Communist "democracy" is in reality a system of rigged organizations whereby the people are made to feel they are taking part in public affairs, when in reality they are simply being manipulated by Party propaganda on a mass scale.

The Communists foster a form of government *for* the people rather than *of* and *by* the people. Such government is in keeping with the best interests of the people as their interests are defined by the Party. Consequently, Communist leaders perceive themselves to be caretakers of the people. They have full authority to decide what is best, as well as full coercive power to enforce their decisions and to punish all deviations from the established norm.

These limitations in the Communist understanding of the democratic process afford a basis for evaluating their concept of the state. The Overstreets insist that "the Soviet Union is not a modern state." No state is exclusively modern, but those that best qualify for the name have wrought into their common life and institutions certain concepts: "The inviolable worth of the individual; the right of dissent; freedom of the mind to search for truth and to express its findings; freedom of religion; freedom of the press; freedom of association; respect for the social contribution of diversity; respect for the role of a loyal opposition; liberty under law; and the sovereignty of the people." [8] The Soviet Union and the Chinese Communist state are totalitarian, monolithic states in which a self-appointed elité exact the fullest possible measures of devotion from their subjects. The Communists perceive those states which best demonstrate the above-mentioned modern qualities as their worst enemies because they allow free exercise of the human faculties, and because they contradict the

---

[8] Overstreet, *op. cit.,* p. 66.

claim of communism to be an elect agent of a fated historical process which affords the only possible line of advance for mankind.

In this brief review of the Communist challenge, special attention has been given to the effects of the Marxian ideology upon man and his capacity to live in qualitative relation to other persons in society. The intolerable exclusivism of the system has been exposed. It has been noted that communism destroys both the ability and the desire of Communist man to enter into relation with other persons except on Communist terms. It is at the point of this impassé in the crucial area of human relations that Christianity can best assault communism. It is here that the Christian concept of community comes to bear. The "We-Thou" nature of the Christian fellowship constitutes the main thrust of a true Christian understanding of society. This means persons living under God and in community so that each is perceived as unique and vital to the livelihood and well-being of the whole. This fundamental difference between Christianity and communism should afford some practical bases for determining the lines of Christian strategy in opposing the Marxist system.

The Appeals of the Challengers

Effective strategy depends in part upon an understanding of the nature of the appeal made by the opposition. If Christians are to meet the Communist challenge effectively, they must have a clear grasp of those elements in communism which have made it attractive to so many people. Some attention will now be given to several elements in the very real Communist appeal.

A closed rational system.—Communism has the intellectual appeal of a closed rational system. There is a certain undeniable attraction in a thought system which has all the answers. Communism, at least in theory, is just such a system. The determinism derived from the "scientific" nature of the movement utilizes the so-called inevitabilities of the material universe. Through its concept of economic determinism, communism presents a view of history wherein everything is ultimately determined by materialistic inevitabilities. Such a view affords the Marxists their concept of co-operation with history and leads them to the conclusion that history is on their side.

Communism is more than an idea or a philosophy; it is basically *a way of life*. It affords a rational explanation of God, man, and the universe as well as history, economics, government, and society. It affords a closed system. Once a person assumes the mental stance of the Marxist, all the pieces of the puzzling universe fall into place. All of life becomes materialized and thus predictable and controllable. The appeal of communism is based, to a considerable degree, upon the need of mankind for a unifying force in life. There has been a marked tendency in some quarters to distinguish sharply between the sacred and the secular sphere of experience, thus dividing the loyalties and practices of the individual into well-defined compartments. Communism is the strongest contemporary manifestation of the breakdown of this dichotomy. It results in the complete secularization of all of life. In the process, however, it provides a basis for the unification of life. This constitutes its practical intellectual appeal.

Maston has described dialectical materialism as "predestination with God left out." It materializes all of life and interprets the whole of reality from this vantage point. The fundamental difference between Christianity and communism at this point is in the relative significance of the material. Christianity in the main has fostered "a spiritualized materialism." That is a materialism which recognizes the significance of material values but keeps them always in proper subordination to spiritual values.

In its view of history communism provides an end without a consummation. The end of all temporal striving is the classless society. If this utopian dream should ever be accomplished the Communists have no more to say. For them history stops there. The best they can afford, therefore, is some faraway fairy tale land where collectivized human beings settle down to live happily ever after. In its view of history, communism suffers the same fault as all those rational systems which insist that a single category is sufficient to explain the whole of the happenings through the ages, and that a single vantage point provides the exclusive key for a systematic analysis of all events.

The Communists' relativistic ethic is determined by their fundamental world view. They define the good in terms of its contribution to their goals in history. Their goal is proletarian revolution which leads ultimately to a classless society. Any method is employed so long as it contributes to the achievement of their goals, both immediate and long-range. Any means is justified by the end.

An urgent plan of action.—Communism affords the emotional appeal of an urgent plan of action. It is a system with a plan for world conquest. Anyone who reads the *Communist Manifesto* comes away with at least the conviction that here is a movement convinced both of the "rightness" of its cause and the inevitability of its triumph. This world is a place where entirely too many persons eat too little, live too wretchedly, suffer too severely, and die too young. Any voice that offers a way out of these conditions is going to be heard. Communism is such a voice. Communism attracts generally because its goals are more to be desired than its methods are to be immediately feared. Communists are certain that mankind possesses the ability to control its own destiny. They believe with passion that they are leading mankind out of capitalistic darkness toward an existence in which poverty, misery, and wars will be unknown except in history books. They miss no opportunity to inspire men to action.

Communists are gripped by a sense of urgency. They are out to right the wrongs in the world and they must get on with the business at hand. For persons who perceive themselves as co-operating with the inevitabilities of history they manifest a peculiar restlessness. In the summer of 1960, during his visit to Austria, Nikita Khrushchev said, "Life is short, and I want to see the Red flag fly over the whole world in my lifetime." If he fails, it is quite likely that no other Communist dictator will have that satisfaction. It is obvious from repeated public statements by Communist leaders that there is a growing conviction upon the part of Marxists that the world balance of power is shifting in their favor. Conversely, they believe the United States and her allies are losing influence and power in world affairs.

In a speech, termed by experts to be his *Mein Kampf,* delivered January 6, 1961, Khrushchev reaffirmed both the goals and plan of action which the Communists will project for the next five years or so. It is his opinion that the final decision in the world struggle, and specifically the victory of international communism, will be attained in the present era of history. In his mind, this era extends to approximately 1975. The turning point in the present struggle will come when the Soviet Union overtakes the United States sometime between 1965 and 1970. Such a condition will prevail when the Soviet Union, irrespective of per capita production in industrial or consumer goods, achieves technologically superior armaments and attains a military force which will be qualitatively and quantitatively superior to the military force of the United States.

The over-all economic goal of communism consists of the public's ownership and control of the basic means of production, distribution, and credit. As a means to this end, the Communists at present embrace at least four strategic objectives: Fragmentation of the West, neutralization of emerging nations, isolation and encirclement of the United States, and the continual sapping of capitalism's economic, cultural, and political foundations. In a world where the majority of people are miserable in their struggle against poverty, hunger, disease, unemployment, illiteracy, inequalities, oppression, and war, the Communists' exactness as to a plan of action and their confidence in the workability of this plan carries tremendous emotional power.

A worthy cause.—There is inherent in communism the religious appeal of a cause worthy of man's best efforts. In spite of the fact that communism denies any point of reference outside of the material world, thus refusing to accept the existence of God, the human soul, or eternal life, it is in the final analysis a religion. This is true because it affords man a framework for the understanding of himself, his world, and his place in the world. It has a formulated body of teachings about the purpose of life in the world, both as individuals and society. Moreover, communism captures a man's ultimate concern and demands his absolute loyalty. It provides its adherents with a faith to live by, a program for facing their problems, and a hope in the final establishment of an ideal society. Anything that affords all these benefits, while trying to answer the fundamental problems of life, must be regarded as a religion.

In a fine analysis of communism as it is contrasted to Christianity, Charles W. Lowry calls the two "conflicting faiths." [9] There is little room to doubt that, for the present at least, communism is the most militant and challenging faith that faces Christianity. The Communists believe their kingdom is at hand. With all deliberate haste they are "evangelizing" the world with a missionary zeal perhaps unparalleled in history by any except the early Christians, the militant Moslems, and the Hitler-inspired fascists.

T. B. Maston has drawn attention to two very serious limitations in communism as a religion. One is its failure to take death seriously. Human life is far too cheap to the Marxists. In their failure to take death seriously, they fail to provide their adherents with the resources to meet life's most certain and, for many, its most grim reality. The

---

[9] *Conflicting Faiths: Christianity Versus Communism* (Washington: Public Affairs Press, 1953).

other weakness is the Communists' failure to rid themselves of hatred for those outside their group. It is an undeniable fact that hatred for those outside one's group tends to damage and ultimately to destroy the sense of fellowship within the group. Berdyaev has said that "the preponderance of hate over love is terrible among Communists."[10]

For Christians there can be no significant community apart from love. God, who is *agape* love, engenders love of like quality in all humans who partake of his nature through Jesus Christ. Only such love, which exerts itself, regardless of the worth of the one loved and worthwhileness of the affection, can last and live. Society built on anything less will ultimately collapse from the inside. "Better is a dinner of herbs where love is, than a stalled ox and hatred therewith" (Prov. 15:17).

Successful system.—Communism holds the pragmatic appeal of a system that works. Measured by certain self-contained standards, communism is obviously a success. The economic condition of large segments of mankind has been substantially altered. Whole societies have been changed by revolutionary means. These achievements have made an indelible impression on the world's "down-and-outs." The chaotic conditions in Europe and Asia following two world wars have proved to be fallow ground for the Communist advance. Their willingness to use brute force while ignoring every principle of ethics and law has contributed to their success. Through their ability to adjust their tactics to ever-changing conditions, Communist leaders have added vast areas of land and people to their camp. Their attitude is an uncompromising one which brooks no rivals. This gives to the movement a homogeneity unknown to most other power systems.

Measured by purely materialistic standards, Communist achievements in Russia, China, and the satellites have been of no small consequence. Obviously, communism has succeeded in many ways in these countries. However, if communism is judged by what it has done to men, women, and children—to persons in relation—then the record is not so good.

In Russia, for example, a great social class has been created by the methods of exile, imprisonment, and compulsion. Believing that the discipline of labor refines and reforms human life, the Soviets have mobilized a vast army of forced laborers. The number of persons

---

[10] Nicolas Berdyaev, *The Origin of Russian Communism* (London: Geoffrey Bles, 1955), p. 184.

subjected to such labor in Russia is impossible to determine, but the fact that many millions are so exploited is no longer questionable. Without the armies of forced laborers the Russian state economy could never have achieved the phenomenal growth so much in evidence.

In the process of collectivization of the Russian peasantry the kulaks, the more well-to-do and intelligent peasants, have been virtually annihilated by slaughter and exile. Likewise, since the war, five small Russian republics with a population estimated in excess of three million have been abolished for political reasons. The people once comprising these republics have been either slain or deported to out-of-the-way labor camps.

Undeniable strides toward a better standard of living for millions of the Russian population have been taken. These strides take on a new dimension, however, when one considers the vast number of slave laborers who struggled to make them realizable. Moreover, the east European satellites have been drained of raw materials and installations in the process of improving the economy of the Soviet Union. Then, too, substantial quantities of industrial equipment and technological know-how were channeled to Russia from the United States. Before, during, and after World War II, vast amounts of goods were exported to the Soviet Union, much of it in the nature of Lend-Lease assistance. The value of most of this material has never been repaid. Still another factor to be considered is the undeniable contribution made to Russian science and technology by German and other experts who were taken to the Soviet Union following the war. To recognize the achievements of these does not mean that Russia's own scientists and technicians have not been creative and successful in their own right.

The Communists dramatically pose as champions of so-called "target peoples." From the Marxist perspective the emerging nations of Africa and Asia are prizes to be gained in the world power struggle. On the other hand the free world perceives these nations not primarily as units to be added to an expanding power bloc, but as free republics which must have their independence and right to self-determination so underwritten by the strength of the United Nations and the free world that no great power bloc can infringe upon them or exploit them. It was Hammarskjöld's position on this point that brought Khrushchev's wrath down upon his head.

The emerging nations have posed one of communism's gravest problems. Marxist leaders have made it quite clear that they are ready to give aid to any progressive element that seizes power in any country. In each case where they have moved in, however, their problem has been to make their support of such elements look convincingly like an effort to help the new nation find its way to a just, stable, and creative independence. In every situation the Communists have soon shown their true color. A discriminating observer can detect that "no matter how 'peaceful' their first approach may be, they cannot achieve their purpose without acting like Communists: which is to say, without trying to gain coercive control." [11]

A flexible strategy.—Communism affords the tactical appeal of a strategy that can be swiftly changed. This is an advantage enjoyed by a dictatorship operating within the context of a planned economy rather than a free economy. The Communists have attracted worldwide attention due to the nature of their system which enables them to throw a large segment of their resources and efforts behind any one desired project. Whereas the intricacies of the democratic process in a free society determine to some degree the speed by which a tactical decision affecting the whole economy can be made, Communist leaders suffer no such handicap. Their policy is decreed by fiat command.

The Communists' ability to mobilize resources quickly in order to foster any desired project has made Russia an imposing national power. The emphasis on science and technology has had obvious results. A world looking on, accustomed to assessing only the tangible evidences of progress, has been duly impressed. For many people it is of little consequence that, in spite of the phenomenal advance in Soviet industrialization, at present a man-hour worked in Russia is exchangeable for only about one-eighth of the goods and services that a man-hour in the United States represents.

Military might.—The final Communist appeal to be mentioned is that of sheer numbers and military might. The very facts that one-third of the world's population is under direct or indirect Marxist control and that Communist leaders can order a fifty-megaton nuclear bomb exploded, or mobilize what is perhaps numerically the largest army in the world, or fire a rocket to the moon, or put a man-carrying

---

[11] Overstreet, *op. cit.*, p. 96.

satellite into orbit around the earth cannot help but impress friends, enemies, and neutrals.

In light of these appeals it becomes evident that the free world and Christians more particularly are up against a materialistic philosophy that makes its appeal to the bread-hunger and power-hunger of the world, obsessed with a dream of world domination and driven by something that is akin to a religious zeal.

In spite of their triumph over a third of the earth's people and a fourth of the earth's surface, there is a growing number of persons who are convinced that communism is a colossal failure. With all their long opportunity to capitalize on the chaos of war-torn Europe, as well as the discontents and mutual antagonism of men and nations, coupled with their chances to tap the hopes, idealisms, and unsuspicious decencies of these nations, still the Communists have never won a country by free election. They triumph by conspiracy, subversion, free world credulity, and naked force. They must continuously cover up the fact that in no country where they have seized power has the Party been able to bring about a state of affairs in which it can let down its guard and rely on the support of the people.

The record speaks for itself. In open competition with other systems communism cannot prove its case to the minds and consciences of men. In view of such a "failure" many believe that if Christians and the free world can hold firm for another decade or so, putting its creative mind to work on problems attendant upon freedom's advance, it may become too late for communism to add further victories.

A Strategy for Meeting the Challenge

There is, of course, no clear-cut, neatly outlined, easily implemented strategy whereby Christianity can defeat communism in this generation. Likewise, it is a fatal misjudgment to identify Christian strategy with the strategy of the free world in dealing with Marxism. It is to be hoped that the latter will be governed by the principle of the former, but there is little ground for assuming this to be the case at the present time.

Unquestionably, there is a basis for describing Christianity as the "ultimate weapon" against communism. There is a danger, however, that in the thinking of some people Christianity should become merely a tool for use in the power struggle. There never has been, nor will there ever be, any justification for persons to embrace Christianity simply in an effort to defeat communism or any other evil on a world scale. On the positive side Christianity, too, is a way of life—the greatest the world has ever known—involving God's reign in the total life of man and society. Through the centuries whenever and wherever Christians have been assessed for what they are, void of any and all nationalistic, imperialistic, or cultural trappings, they have impressed the world's people with their quality of life.

In the Christian world of spiritual supremacy man is a creature of God. He is made in God's image, bearing the spiritual qualities of his nature. As such, man has personal, temporal, and eternal value. Man is not made for the state; the state is made for man—as is everything in the material world. It is man's to learn to use in keeping with the will and purpose of the Creator. This is the Christian view of life. When believed and shared voluntarily, this view of life and the world can do more for man than the Marxist world view.

Christians are not going to meet the challenge of world communism if they use no power except that known to Communists. Missiles lead to antimissiles, and that to anti-antimissiles. Where does the arms race stop? Christians possess a power—or they are possessed by a power—that is not of human or material origin. It is the power of God in Christ made evident by self-authenticating events in history. This power can change a man. Back of it and in it is God's redemptive purpose in history and beyond history.

Even the brief analysis afforded by this chapter reveals that communism is half-truth and positive error. In spite of this fact, Christians must leave a place in their thinking for a nation, exercising its right of free determination, to choose communism as its means of national economic expression. This means simply that Christianity does not direct its main criticism of communism at its major objective or at the social, economic, and political programs it uses to attain those objectives. Christians, then, must not make the mistake of placing communism over against capitalism in such a way as to condemn the first *in toto* and defend *in toto* the latter. Many have sought to do this and have made their case weak and often ridiculous. However, Christians must be critical of communism's economic and political program at two fundamental points. First, it claims too much. It makes of its program an all-encompassing world view that becomes for its adherents the supreme value of their lives. Second, it claims to free people while, in fact, it actually enslaves them. Individuals lose their identity and worth in the group and are sacrificed, if need be, for the program and the Party.

In outlining an effective strategy for meeting the Communist challenge on a world scale Christians, as well as the entire free world, must review, purify, and if necessary change their motives. Since the Communist opinion of the West has been ideologically defined a long time ago—and for keeps—it appears that the best procedure is for the free world to match its policies with its own beliefs about the nature of man and his life in society, rather than to trim and shape them in the hope that the Communists can be persuaded to credit the good intentions.

Any and all actions of the free world will be propagandized and denounced as subtle plans for the enslavement and exploitation of persons. Therefore, motives for our giving aid, as for our other undertakings, need to be understood both by ourselves and other free world nations and peoples who have a stake in them.

There are some rather definite ways *not* to meet the Communist challenge. The Overstreets examine some means whereby Christians and the free world can hand over to Khrushchev in his lifetime the makings of final Communist victory. All of these ways are described as "ways of self-indulgence" because each represents a selective evasion of issues. The first way to fail in meeting the Communist challenge is through a self-indulgent pessimism which concludes that communism is here to stay. Such a view confuses the colossal and monolithic with the strong, and wrongly assesses history as an inexorable process rather than one being made what it is by divine and human interaction within temporal events.

A second way to fail in facing up to the Communist challenge is through a self-indulgent optimism which declares that industrialization and rising living standards in the Soviet Union are bound to alter communism and eventually have a liberalizing effect upon the Russian people. Such a view differs from pessimism only in its conclusion that fate is prone to deliver happy endings. Aside from the fact that it does not recognize the full implications of Communist theology, this view diminishes man to a being to whom things happen without his assuming any responsibility for the incident.

A third way to fail in meeting the Communist challenge is through a self-indulgent sentimentality which encourages unilateral disarmament or disarmament on Communist terms, thereby leaving the entire free world at the mercy of a militant and fully armed foe. Generally, those embracing such a view argue that it would be better "Red than dead." Such a position has to be rated as profoundly immoral.

Still another way to fail in facing the Communist threat is through a self-indulgent indifference which tires of hearing about the problem. Human needs and aspirations must be recognized. The clamor in a world of wretched people will be heard; it must be heeded! Both knowledge of the conditions and compassion for the people are necessary if communism is to be defeated.

A fifth way to fail in meeting the Communist challenge is to rely entirely upon a negative approach. Surely, any thinking Christian is against communism. However, merely being anti-Communist is not enough. John F. Kennedy denounced "the councils of fear and suspicion" emanating from various far-right fringe groups in this country and in Europe. He warned against hunting treason in the courts and churches and joining movements that are more likely to produce local vigilantes than national vigilance. Dwight D. Eisenhower has added that the United States needs no "superpatriots." Maston observes that "when opposing communism Christian groups should not permit themselves to become identified with other movements that would destroy or at least dilute and undermine the Christian movement." [12]

How, then, can Christians meet the Marxist challenge? What are some elements in an effective strategy? A neat and easy answer is not possible.

Communism, from the Christian perspective, is essentially another form of evil expressing itself with fearsome power on a world scale. It is not the first such manifestation of evil. It will probably not be the last. Christians once more are called upon to recapture the dynamics and strategy of the New Testament community. They cannot afford to go on fighting a kind of rear-guard action while the Communists "call the plays" around the world. Christians must develop a bold strategy of their own. They must be *for* something, give more of themselves to the cause of Christ, and implement their faith with courage and enthusiasm. Christians must remember that an adequate answer to communism must go deeper and be broader than economic benefits, political advantages, or military strategy.

---

[12] *Op. cit.*, p. 195.

Christians must attack communism at its weakest points. The fundamental weakness of the Marxist system is its effects on human beings—both as individuals and in social relationships. It is here that Christianity has a real opportunity to counteract communism and eventually to defeat it. An effort has been made throughout this chapter to show what happens to a person when he is transformed into a Communist man.

Communists commit the worst possible sin against a man. They capture him with a lie. They promise that society will pass rather quickly through its socialistic phase, that the state will wither away, that religion in the usual sense will no longer be needed, and that society will inevitably become classless. They have progressively put off the day of carrying out these promises to their own people. Marx expected the big change immediately. Lenin said it would require thirty years. Stalin said it would take many generations—perhaps a thousand years. Khrushchev has said that the pure communistic phase will be impossible to attain so long as the Soviet Union is threatened by the capitalistic encirclement. The Communists in 1917 promised equality for all. It is now a crime in Russia to talk about equality. New class distinctions have developed to be sure, but equality is no nearer actualization than under the czars. As they rose to power, the Marxists had a great passion for liberty. They promised freedom for all who would follow them. Today, to make the Communist system effective in Europe, a secret police force (the MVD) has been created. It is far more fearsome than the police of the czar.

Christians need to remind the world that during the time since World War II—the period corresponding to the greatest thrust of Soviet empire building—the Western colonial powers have granted independence to more than 750 million persons in thirty nations, and that still other nations and people are slated for independence within the next several months. The Soviet Union now rules over forty-nine colonial and semicolonial territories. These peoples are not free to choose their own political forms or to establish their own economic systems. If they attempted to do so, like Hungary, they would quickly feel the effects of Soviet power. This Russian-type colonialism must be exposed. It is perpetrated by one of three strategic systems—revolution from within, revolution from without, or revolution from above through coalition government. Neither of these has tactical precedence.

Perhaps a vigorous and well administered program of exchange on several levels would prove one of the best possible means currently for Christians to prevent the Soviet-bloc citizen from being made into Communist man. The aim of such exchange has been well defined as an effort to keep the future roomy enough for creative developments to take place within the orbit with the individual, morally responsible human mind as a prime mover. Christian churches generally could participate in an effective way in such exchange programs.

Since no one knows what form Communist desperation may take at any point when its "fated" victory turns out not to be so automatic, Christians will do well to see to it that their well-rounded strategy is such that any resort to all-out war initiated by the Communists is kept inexpedient. It is generally agreed that Christians are often forced, in light of all the factors in a given situation, to incorporate elements in their strategy which in ideal or even different situations would be quite different. Such is the case in combating communism on a world scale. Therefore, an effective well-rounded Christian strategy should include provision for a military deterrent against Communist aggression.

The Communists have one fear that outranks all others—"the fear that the free nations will unite and stay united." Consequently, Christians can endorse and hope for the realization of a strong political confederation of free nations, along with a free world trade organization, which will monitor trade so as to develop backward countries and strengthen the free democracies.

Christians are engaged in a war of ideas. These respect no boundaries, culture, race, or class. They can reach and alter the minds and spirits of men. Therefore, Christians can support any worthy effort to train persons from all nations in the art of ideological warfare, i.e., battling communism in the arena of ideas.

All of these considerations, however, are preliminary to the fundamental element in a Christian strategy for meeting the Communist challenge. That is a revitalization of Christianity. Christians must remember that ultimate victory of God in Christ is one thing. The victory of Christianity in its present state of health is quite another. A genuine repentance and sincere faith are basic not just as tools to combat communism but as means in the creation of genuine Christian community. Christians everywhere must take an honest look at their own spiritual health. Are they matching the Communists in commitment? Do they care enough about their fellowman—regardless of race or nationality—to make democracy a reality? Do they know how to "hate causes and love people"—to distinguish between the evil of communism and the people who have become subjected to its tyranny? Before Christians can meet the challenge of communism there are some things they must let God set straight in their thinking and living. "Christians must be challenged to outlive, outlove, and if need be outdie the communists." [13]

Yet, diagnosis is not cure. There are at least three specific areas of revitalization desperately needed in contemporary Christianity. First, Christians must recover sensitivity. A cold war creates cold hearts. Suspicions, indifference, and misunderstanding are rife among men. Christians must recapture the Master's concern for those who need help—both for bread and the Bread of life. This concern must be implemented by the material help which they are able to give. It does little good to tell a man about the love of God if his hunger for bread can be relieved and Christians take no significant steps to do so. The fundamental thrust in Christianity is one's right relation to God. But an inevitable corollary is his right relation to his fellowman. The vertical and the horizontal dimensions of the Christian faith must ever remain in constant tension, proper relation, and practical balance. Christians must combat with all their strength the obvious tendency within organized Christendom to move away from the masses "up to" the middle and upper classes.

In the second place Christians must recognize that sometimes progress does accompany change. They must cease to be afraid to change that which has lived out its purpose in serving either God or man. Too often when Christians speak of the error of communism they speak in terms which vindicate the status quo and all of the things which communism seeks to remedy. The fact is that there are many weaknesses in the status quo. There are many phases of life in the West which are repulsively materialistic and very evidently non-Christian, if not anti-Christian. It is likewise true that through the centuries a sub-Christian status quo has been more often defended than threatened in the name of Christ. Christians must become willing to bring about some radical changes in their lives and society or put themselves in a spiritual frame of mind so that God can.

In the third place Christians must give a new emphasis, new

---

[13] Maston, *op. cit.*, p. 198.

mobility, and new personnel to their whole program of evangelism and world missions. Money and bread alone are not enough. Christians must find ways of sharing the warmth of their personal compassion. They must give more of themselves. This is not to criticize what missionaries have done or are doing, but it is to say that Christians need to do more, do it better, do it with a greater sense of urgency, and find new ways of doing it more effectively. As one Christian missionary has said, "If we are to keep the world from going to the Communists, we must win it to Christ."

The initiative for social change must pass from the Communists to Christians. Communism is making tremendous headway on many frontiers of need. Christians can destroy and displace it only if they come to realize that to be a Christian means to accept a social as well as an individual ethic. The supreme concern for those who suffer injustice can be reborn in the hearts of Christians only when they realize that their faith implies positive action on behalf of others. Here, as in most other phases of Christian strategy, the effectiveness of the operation depends to a very large extent upon the Christian minister.

The Christian minister specifically can do at least two things in meeting the Communist challenge. In the first place he can become informed about the opposition. It would be difficult to exaggerate the widespread lack of knowledge among ministers regarding communism. Generally they know a few facts, but the essential essence and broader implications of Marxism remain a mystery to most of them. Such a situation can and must be remedied.

How can a minister acquire information? A good place to start is with the *Communist Manifesto*. Here Marx and Engels have outlined for the world to see their policies and plan of action. In addition to this brief document most of the writings of Communist leaders from Marx to Khrushchev have been ably translated and are available in inexpensive editions. Besides these original sources there have been many volumes of various worth written to interpret the Communist challenge. A helpful catalog of secondary sources covering a variety of approaches to the subject has been provided by R. N. Carew Hunt.[14] Some of the most current and helpful literature on communism is available from the United States Government Printing Office. A

---

[14] His volume contains nothing but a bibliography and is entitled *Books on Communism* (London: Ampersand, 1959).

biweekly listing of all publications is available upon request. Any minister who has the interest and will take the time can become informed regarding the Communist challenge. Once he has acquired the necessary information, he must play a vital role in apprising others of the dimensions of the challenge.

In the second place a minister can aid in meeting the Marxist threat by pressing the claims of the total Christian gospel upon the total man. This must be done with courage, precision, and enthusiasm. He must press the exciting appeal of the Christian hope, both in its this-worldly and other-worldly aspects. Such hope engenders confidence in the fact that God may seem to lose some battles, but he has never lost a war. Correctly interpreted and applied in lives, Christian hope provides the dynamic for meeting human sin, suffering, and death, and thus fulfils the deepest longing of human hearts everywhere.

Any preaching of the total gospel for the total man must center in the cross and resurrection of Jesus Christ. The Christian answer to communism, or any other competing way of life, involves the cross, both as the focal point of God's redemptive activity and as an ethical dimension to be made manifest in daily worship and work. Life in Christ is life under the cross, since it demonstrates God's loving activity as he redeems and judges all mankind.

Christians can meet the challenge of communism, but it will require their best effort. It will require immediate action coupled with the prayer—

Let us confess our pride of place and station which seeks advantage over other men.

Let us confess our self-centeredness which keeps us from seeking the common good.

Let us confess our slowness to accept as brothers those for whom Christ died.

Let us confess our idolatry which makes a god out of "our cause" while refusing to admit that the One who is with us is also with those who oppose us, loving them as He loves us.[15]

Additional Reading

DALLIN, DAVID J. *The Changing World of Soviet Russia.* New Haven: Yale University Press, 1956.

---

[15] *Church Council Bulletin,* North Carolina Council of Churches, November 15, 1961.

HINDUS, MAURICE. *House Without a Roof*. Garden City: Doubleday &
Co., 1961.

HORDERN, WILLIAM. *Christianity, Communism and History*. New York:
Abingdon Press, 1954.

HUNT, R. N. CAREW. *The Theory and Practice of Communism*. New
York: The Macmillan Co., 1957.

OVERSTREET, HARRY A. and BONARO. *The War Called Peace*. New York:
W. W. Norton & Co., 1961.

9

Censorship and Mass Communication

EDDIE RICKENBAKER

Censorship—the seemingly "dirty" word for many in the field of communication—has become the last alternative for some outside of that field. Recently, a parent and part-time author, who said she had never dreamed of speaking out in favor of censorship, was being forced to do so by the prevailing sex-saturated social climate. Writing in *Today's Health,* she pointed out that "poison" was being given out with pious claims such as, " 'This is honesty. This is freedom. This is art.' Those who protest are referred to in tones of cultured contempt as 'reformers,' 'do-gooders,' 'censors of our liberties,' or 'those who would deprive us of the right to see and hear.' " [1]

The spread of this "poison" was formerly confined to books and magazines. However, movies and television are now being used. The motion picture appeals to the two most vital senses, sight and hearing, at the same time. The effect is potent indeed. The tragedy of this is that movies today are being made from books that seem to contain more and more filth. The "dirtier" the book, it seems, the greater are its chances for financial success and critical acclaim. [2] " 'The only trouble,' complains one novelist who first rose to fame on the sex crest, 'is that it's getting harder and harder to shock people.' " [3]

---

[1] Marjorie Holmes, "A Mother Speaks Up for Censorship," *Today's Health,* XL (January, 1962), 51.

[2] This was not true with regard to the famous (or infamous) "sex book," *Tropic of Cancer.* The book has been censored in various parts of the country and, contrary to popular opinion of many opposed to censorship, this has hurt the sales. Cf. *American Library Association Bulletin,* February, 1962, pp. 81 f.

[3] Holmes, *op. cit.,* p. 66.

These statements and others like them warrant particular attention to the possibility of censorship in the media of mass communication.

Censorship and Freedom

Censorship and freedom are not concepts which automatically stand in opposition to each other, as some have supposed. On the contrary, censorship can have a place in either of the two philosophical views of freedom usually held today.

Freedom—the ability to do as one pleases.—The proponents of this view hold that a man is free only if he acts in the light of his own preferences and decisions. They argue that he is constrained whenever he is limited to one possible course of action, even if the limitation is thought to be justified by someone else's decision concerning what is good or true.

Aristotle and in more recent times Dewey and Holmes, among others in America, have maintained that a man is free only so long as he may make his own choices. If choice is foreclosed by another's judgment about what is virtuous or wise, freedom is lost. According to the proponents of this philosophical approach, the chances of discovering what really is virtuous or wise diminish when to disagree is impossible. Holmes insisted that "the best test of truth is the power of the thought to get itself accepted in the competition of the market." [4] Aristotle had faith "in the value of the individual's own search for virtue and his free action in association with others to secure the common good." [5]

Censorship, to a certain extent, is contained in this view. Whenever a person or a law gets in the way of one's so-called "freedom," that person or law must be obliterated or "censored." Thus, the majority determines what is right and wrong without regard to any higher virtues. In fact, as Holmes pointed out above, truth and virtue are not absolutes but are determined by the majority.

Freedom—the ability to do as one ought.—The proponents of this view hold that only the wise man or the good man is truly free. Therefore, this man is the only one who acts in accordance with his own nature. They argue that a man is not free when he acts under the influence of erroneous ideas or passions. When a man is acting under

---

[4] Walter Gellhorn, "Restraints on Book Reading," *The First Freedom,* ed. Robert B. Downs (Chicago: American Library Association, 1960), p. 21.

[5] *Ibid.*

these influences, his acts are being determined by external circumstances.

Plato, Augustine, and Spinoza, among many others, asserted that no man is free who acts erroneously under the influence of passion or mistaken ideas. When what is true and good is known, anything that would subvert it should be controlled. This control is not to narrow man's freedom, but to save him from the "unfreedom" of immorality or harmful doctrine that might damage him or the community. "In this view censorship rests in one or another degree upon the belief that those who are qualified to identify evil and mistake should be empowered to prevent their dissemination." [6]

Censorship is, therefore, an essential part of this view. It is not so much that a man's freedom will be limited, but that he will be saved from harmful consequences both to himself and to society if he has guidelines within which to use that freedom. In this case the majority does not determine right and wrong but determines who is qualified to judge what is right and wrong. The censor is not self-appointed, else this would approximate dictatorship or, at the best, thought control.

Liberty versus license.—Thus, the matter of freedom "boils down" to the question of liberty or license. When does one's freedom determine his liberty and when does one's freedom become license? Doesn't a man have the right to say or print anything that he wants? He does, according to the Constitution. However, a man does not have the right to distribute the material if the content is of such a nature as to have a detrimental effect on those receiving it.

This principle can be well illustrated when applied to a common vehicle, the automobile. A man has the right to drive his automobile anywhere he chooses as long as he obeys the traffic laws. However, should he exceed the speed limit and endanger the lives of others by his reckless driving, his liberty has become license and he must temporarily be deprived of that liberty.

Taking this principle into the area of social action, a further illustration is seen. A man can legally consume as much alcoholic beverage as he likes. However, he does not have the "right" to get behind the wheel of an automobile in a drunken state because there are laws against driving while intoxicated. There are also laws against indecent exposure which seem not to have been applied when the

---

[6] *Ibid.*

indecent exposure is on the printed page or is shown on the screen.

When lawmakers seek to make these laws effective in the media of mass communication, the cry arises, "Our liberties are being bombarded." Therefore, the difference between liberty and license seems to be slight. However, the distinction must be made. Liberty does not imply license! The whole concept of law is based on the principle of insuring liberty for all but licence for none.

Censorship as Regulation

Censorship and suppression.—In a recent survey an interesting answer was received with regard to the matter of censorship and control. The editor of one of the larger Sunday supplemental magazines pointed out a distinction between the editor's general function of deciding to print or reject certain material and censorship itself, which is an attempt by persons outside the editor's organization to suppress material which he wishes to publish, or has already published.[7] Significant in this answer is the emotional word "suppress." Is censorship, in fact, suppression or is it regulation? Can a distinction be made between regulation and suppression?

The dictionary defines the primary meaning of "control" as power, authority, direction. It defines the primary meaning of "suppression" as a putting down by force or authority; putting an end to. With regard to censorship, the confusion in the meaning of these two terms is very apparent. People who would ordinarily approve regulation of mail by the Post Office Department and regulation of food and drugs by the Department of Health's Pure Food and Drug Act suddenly become infuriated at the mention of censorship and begin to cry "suppression." They begin to quote the Constitution, the Declaration of Independence and other "venerable" documents in their defense.

Undoubtedly, many persons advocating censorship have the destruction of the thing censored as the ultimate objective. The fact that something may be misused by a person, however, does not necessarily mean that it should be destroyed or prohibited. Many things would then be denied which in the hands of the right persons actually benefit mankind. "Unrestrained 'censorship' would undoubtedly result in the

---

[7] A survey on the question of "Censorship in Mass Communication" was made by the author in the spring of 1962. All further references to this survey will be indicated: Survey.

removal of much that could prove to be helpful or good in our society. The good would often be destroyed with the bad." [8]

Censorship and control—There are precedents in our society for regulation or control, rather than suppression, for the protection of the social order. Thus, the question of whether censorship is necessary is a question of the protection of the social order. If it can be proved that materials of mass communication produce antisocial acts, not merely bad thoughts and sinful actions over which society has no control, then censorship is necessary. This problem will be considered in more detail later. It is important first to consider manner and methods of control.

Control can come as action taken *after* publication or production, or as action taken *prior* to publication or production. It is interesting to find that the editor of a magazine some would classify as containing much pornographic material takes the position of favoring action *after* publication. He says that "prior restraint is partly unconstitutional as has been determined in many court cases." [9] (It may be that some think if they can only get their material published there may be a possibility of "getting around" the law.)

However, the manager of a radio station in Dallas, Texas, points out that action taken after publication is mainly police action and may not be altogether desirable. "Censorship is a community force. Police action is a state or governmental force. Centralized or government controls carried to extremes are an evil comparable to the need for censorship in the first place." [10]

It would seem, nevertheless, that if control is necessary the proper procedure would be action taken after publication or production. This method of control does seem to be more in keeping with the Bill of Rights in the Constitution. Thus, it is evident again that any person has the right to produce or publish even obscene or pornographic materials in the privacy of his own home or business establishment. It is when these materials produce antisocial acts that control is necessary.

Censorship and thought control.—The opponents of censorship usually insist that censorship means essentially thought control. Two

---

[8] J. Donald Foster, "Another Side to Censorship," *Christianity Today,* VI (February 2, 1962), 22.

[9] Survey.

[10] *Ibid.*

things are evident at this point: a man can *think* about anything, and it is extremely difficult, if not impossible, to control *what* a man thinks. A man can think about anything, but when he begins to influence and harm others then he must be controlled.

During the Korean War there was much alarm about the possibility that American soldiers were being "brainwashed." The Communists had developed a process whereby they could control a man's actions by constantly pouring into his mind certain materials. The application to the matter of censorship is evident. Censorship is not to control what a man sees or hears himself, but to control what he "feeds" to others. Censorship in this sense is not concerned with production but with distribution. People who are horrified at the possibility of soldiers being "brainwashed" sometimes show little concern for the "brainwashing" that is going on through the media of mass communication.

Confusion is evident when the matter of thought control and censorship is discussed. William Dempsey, an attorney from the District of Columbia, is quoted as saying that "thought control is not the business of government, and that government cannot subject movies and books to censorship unless they result in some evil that the state should control." [11] A statement like this seems to be perfectly evident until it is seen that too fine a distinction is made between thought and action. Is it possible that a person can be shown "antisocial" actions and yet these "antisocial" actions be always relegated to the area of thought and never come out in action? Is it possible, as some psychologists and others have indicated, that a man's thoughts greatly determine his actions?

Are there materials that produce antisocial actions? If so, what are they?

Obscenity and Control

The major part of the material written on censorship today has to do with obscenity in one form or another. It is not too much to say, as was indicated by the results on the survey, that the major concern with regard to censorship in the United States is in this area. Since the flood of obscene and pornographic materials has been during the last few years, the problem of censorship in this area has only recently been raised.

---

[11] John B. Sheerin, "Free Speech and Obscenity Censorship," *Catholic World,* CXCIV (December, 1961), 132.

Definition of obscenity.—Probably the hardest question to answer in this area is, "What is obscenity?" There seems to be no meeting of minds at this point. The United States Supreme Court established a test for obscenity in the Roth case in 1957. Justice Brennan, reading the majority opinion, established this test: "Whether to the average person, applying contemporary community standards, the dominant theme of the material taken as a whole appeals to prurient interest." [12] Material that conforms to this definition, according to the Roth decision, is not protected by the First Amendment. That amendment protects only the communication of ideas that have some conceivable social importance.

Norman St. John-Stevas defines obscenity as "material or writing that deals with sex or the excremental functions in such a way as to outrage the prevailing public opinion." [13]

Others think that "science" should play a significant part in any definition. The editor of a magazine which sometimes contains materials that some would judge "obscene" by almost any standard says that obscenity is "that which is scientifically proven to be harmful to mental health and well-being." [14] It is not clear what science will serve best to determine such a matter.

Thus, the question that needs answering is the one above, "Does reading or viewing obscene materials lead to antisocial action?"

Obscenity and behavioral patterns.—The "professionals" are not agreed as to the effect of obscene material on behavior. A panel discussion sponsored by a Catholic group in the latter part of 1961 revealed that many psychiatrists deny that one can prove a causal relationship between reading pornography and sex crimes. It was pointed out that courts proceed on the assumption that reading obscenity does cause these crimes, but "the conscientious jurist is reluctant to convict a news vendor on the strength of a dubious presumption that is under attack from psychiatrists." [15]

On the other hand, recent testimony of psychiatrists, juvenile court judges, law enforcement officials, and clergymen before Congressional

---

[12] Jerome Frank, "United States v. Roth," *The First Freedom, op. cit.*, pp. 119 f.

[13] "The Author's Struggles with the Law," *Catholic World*, CXCIV (March, 1962), 345.

[14] Survey.

[15] Sheerin, *op. cit.*, p. 133.

committees and elsewhere, has shown the serious moral and criminal consequences of obscenity.

E.g., chief neuropsychiatrist Nicholas Frignito of Philadelphia's Municipal Court stated to a House subcommittee his court has case histories of criminal behavior, including homicide, resulting from sexual arousal due to "smutty" books. "Some of these children," he said, did not transgress sexually until they read suggestive stories and viewed lewd pictures or licentious magazines. . . . The filthy ideas implanted in their immature minds impelled them to crime." [16]

Obscenity portrayed as fiction.—Some have contended that "portrayals of such [obscene] material are only fiction, and should not be regarded in the same fashion as educational instruments which must be realistic and true-to-life in their expression of things." [17] Allen Tate, a creative writer, testifying in a Massachusetts court, asked, "Is a literary work of high merit to be condemned because it presents odious language?" [18]

However, if obscenity is only fiction and not to be viewed as factual, it is hard for the viewers and readers always to make this distinction, especially when confronted with a steady stream of this sort of thing. It has a kind of "brainwashing" effect after awhile. The editor of the *Saturday Evening Post* recently pointed this out in an editorial on the subject of obscenity. "Talk to the students in creative-writing courses in any American college, and you will quickly discover that many of them are convinced that no novel is much good unless it contains the frankest possible discussion of sexual matters, in lavatory language." [19]

Obscenity portrayed as a way of life.—There are some who defend obscenity as portraying realism. They say that this is the way life is today and the novelist who uses obscene and pornographic materials is merely being true to life. In defense of such novels as *Lady Chatterley's Lover,* therefore, it has been argued that the book describes the way people live in society today, and to pretend that such things do not in fact exist is to be pietistic to say the least.

Actually, however, as the editor of the *Saturday Evening Post*

---

[16] Quoted in "Eutychus and His Kin," *Christianity Today,* VI (March 16, 1962), 19.

[17] Foster, *op. cit.,* p. 22.

[18] "Judges of Obscenity," *New Republic,* November 27, 1961, p. 7.

[19] "After Obscenity, What?" *Saturday Evening Post,* February 17, 1962, p. 80.

further pointed out, authors are beginning more and more not even to use this defense. "They used to say that they were only 'holding the mirror up to nature,' but this justification won't work for the kind of thing being written today. All of us know at least a few persons who go for days, or even weeks, without uttering at a dinner party even one of the words that are the hallmark of the modern novelist." [20]

Even if this is the way a large number of people do in fact live (which is a questionable proposition), does this alone justify the usage of such a theme in so unrestrained a fashion and with such vulgar language? Is there no ethical code above or beyond what people may do in real life? Can the indiscriminate and unlimited distribution of such material be justified? The matter of distribution is the major matter of concern.

Obscenity portrayed as art.—Some have attempted to defend pornographic and obscene material as a form of literature or art. This would seem to be a position that would be difficult to support. "Examination of the material reveals it to be uniformly lacking in theme, composition, and in general aesthetic quality. Furthermore, the photography is frequently poor and also in poor taste. The desired effect is quite obvious—nothing but lust." [21]

This was so obvious to a group of college students that recently in writing a paper on Hugh Hefner, the editor of *Playboy* magazine, they used as their topic, "The House that Sex Built." Certainly, art forms are not primarily to be used to portray sex, nor should they ever be for that purpose. Neither should art be used primarily to make a profit. Yet, it seems that both the sex motive and, obviously, the profit motive seem to be behind much of the material put out today as art.

Subversion and Control

In another aspect of the matter, concern about obscenity merges into a more generalized concern about dangerous thinking. A Congressional committee, for example, has denounced a book that apparently made a serious argument in favor of polygamy, and entered another into its records because the author "is obviously trying to cash in on the Scottsboro pro-Negro agitation which was Communist-inspired." [22]

---

[20] *Ibid.*

[21] Foster, *op. cit.*, p. 23.

[22] Gellhorn, *op. cit.*, p. 26.

Elsewhere, obscenity has been detected not so much in the wording as in the content of challenges to commonly accepted convictions about the desirability of chastity or monogamy. "In such instances books are censorially threatened because they are the repositories of ideas deemed injurious to society, or, to put it in the more common speech of the day, because they are subversive." [23] Opinions thought to be potentially subversive in the matter of government should always be censored. Even so, materials that are thought to be subversive to the established social and moral order are also to be censored. Thus, it is evident that the censorship of obscenity and the censorship of seditious propaganda are seen to have a common core.

Since the end of World War II, no issue has split the American people more or caused more repercussions than the question of subversion. When is subversion real and when merely imagined? What is the difference between legitimate criticism of governmental actions and procedures and giving aid and comfort to the enemy? Are charges of subversion, so freely thrown about in recent years by officials in high and low places, solidly based or simply devices to gain political advantage? These and other questions must be answered when we look at subversion.

Subversion or dissent.—The recent concern over what one has called the "muzzling of the military" has made us aware of the problems of distinguishing between subversion and dissent. Robert McNamara, secretary of defense, stated to the Senate Armed Services:

> We believe that the military establishment is an instrument, not a shaper, of national policy. Its members, as free Americans, are entitled to their views on the issues of the day, and they have every right to make their views effective through the ballot. They do not have the right, however, to use the military establishment to advance partisan concepts or to alter the decisions of the elected representatives of the people. [24]

The editor of *Saturday Evening Post* concluded, "It is absolutely necessary that the public statements of our military men and other Government officials be 'censored,' reviewed, edited or coordinated. Otherwise the Government will speak with a thousand tongues, and a sensible coordinated policy will not be possible." [25]

---

[23] *Ibid.*
[24] "On 'Muzzling' the Military," *Saturday Evening Post,* March 24, 1962, p. 98.
[25] *Ibid.*

These statements seem to make the matter clear, but when examined closely there seem to be some fallacies. It is not quite true that the military is an "instrument" and not a "shaper" of national policy. Ideally, this would be so, but with the "arms race" moving as fast as it is, it would seem that the military does in fact influence some governmental decisions. If this is so, would it not be only right for the military to have a voice in shaping this policy? Is there such fear of a militaristic state that the military is denied its rightful voice? It seems possible that if a "sensible co-ordinated policy" is formulated without the "thousand tongues" of advisers, possibly even including military advisers, then a dictatorship may be close. Cannot the old adage, "Two heads are better than one," be applied here also?

The confusion in the area of subversion or dissent was shown at a time when General Edwin Walker was put "under pressure" by the Army for trying to indoctrinate his troops in a certain political position. Only a few months later one of his aides was put "under pressure" for giving almost the same propaganda to a group sponsored by the Daughters of the Confederacy. Now it would seem that trying to indoctrinate soldiers and trying to indoctrinate a private group would not be the same offense. Is not freedom of speech before any private group an inalienable right? Is not this different from trying to influence soldiers who are employed by the government to protect that government? In other words, is subversion more dangerous in some cases than in others?

Subversion and security.—The question above is the essential one in the matter of subversion and the possibility of control. There is no one rule that will apply in all cases. There is no doubt about the fact and the gravity of the present crisis in national security. As the leader of the free world, the United States is in the midst of an armament race with the Soviet Union. This is a race with "no holds barred." Therefore, it is evident that anything that would hinder in the race should be stopped. Any materials that would undermine the government should be censored.

How can subversion be determined and eliminated? Walt Kelly, in Keen Satire, has depicted the fascist approach. His "Pogo" some time ago featured the following exchange:

> The Mole: I won't threaten you, Mr. Owl. But here is a book that says: "Owls migrate north about April first. . . . You got a day to pack."

Owl: Why, *you* jes' writ *that* you' ownself. . . .
            Where is Captain Wimby's Bird Atlas?
The Mole: *Dis*credited. It didn't agree with *our* observations. . . .
            Did it, men?
I Cowbird: No sir, it's out of date.
II Cowbird: *And* on fire.
The Mole: There's nothing quite so lovely as a brightly burning
            book.[26]

It would be ridiculous, of course, but, we could follow that approach. Is it ridiculous, however, as some opponents of censorship suggest, to think that subversion can be eliminated without resorting to the Mole's techniques?

It seems that when the security of the country is threatened the proper method of control should be delegated to elected representatives—the House of Representatives and the Senate. They are in a better position to determine subversive threats, having firsthand information that is not available to all.

The Subversive Activities Control Act recently passed by the House of Representatives seems to be the best answer to the problem of subversion and security. The preamble of this bill "declares its justification to be that of protecting American institutions and the nation itself from infiltration by those who would establish a totalitarian dictatorship." [27] This bill was sponsored by the House Committee on Un-American Activities, an important committee in the constant fight against subversion.

Subversion and the "Right Wing."—Possibly a word should be said about the "right-wing" movements today which are violently anti-Communist. Some of those who have cried the loudest for "freedom" and "liberty" are willing to deny it when a "John Bircher" begins to speak. It is certainly as wrong to attach guilt by association in this area, condemning all anti-Communists, as it is to attach such guilt to all who may have had some vague connection with Communists in the past.

The Mechanics of Control

No "cure-all" is here proposed. However, it does seem that certain principles are necessary in effective censorship by control. Control is necessary and possible both for minorities and for the majority.

---

[26] *The Pogo Papers* © 1952–53 Walt Kelly. By permission.
[27] Julian P. Boyd, "Subversive of What?" *The First Freedom*, p. 227.

Control by the minority.—Father John Murray, an outstanding Catholic spokesman, has written an article, "Literature and Censorship," in which he suggests certain principles for control by a minority group. These principles are for the guidance of censoring bodies in a pluralist society.

1. Within the larger pluralist society each minority group has the right to censor for its own members, if it so chooses, the content of the various media of communication, and to protect them, by means of its own choosing from materials considered harmful according to its own standards.
2. In a pluralist society no minority group has the right to demand that government should impose a general censorship, affecting all the citizenry, upon any medium of communication, with a view to punishing the communication of materials that are judged to be harmful according to the special standards held within one group.
3. Any minority group has the right to work toward the elevation of standards of public morality in the pluralist society, through the use of the methods of persuasion and pacific argument.
4. In a pluralist society no minority group has the right to impose its own religious or moral views on other groups, through the use of the methods of force, coercion, or violence.[28]

It is clearly evident that liberty cannot be maintained unless the rights of the minority, as well as the majority, are respected. These minimum rights seem to be necessary in the common interest of social peace.

These rights are based on the supposition that what is commonly imposed by law on all citizens should be supported by general public opinion. Laws should at least be supported by a majority of the whole community. Within a pluralistic society minority groups have certain definite, if limited, rights. These rights include the ability to influence the standards and content of public morality.

It is further to be pointed out that the voluntary association of these minority groups in the public interest is both necessary and desirable. Such groups concern themselves actively with matters that relate to the public welfare. It is not fair to characterize all such groups as "pressure groups," pursuing "private interests." The fact is that, in their own way, they can perform a public function.

---

[28] John Courtney Murray, "Literature and Censorship," *The First Freedom*, pp. 219–20.

It is important to note, however, that the most difficult question concerns the methods used by these groups. There can be no quarrel when they use simply methods of persuasion. Agreement on methods which imply coercion is not so easy. It will certainly be agreed that the use of formal coercion in society is reserved to public authority and law agencies. However, it would seem that coercion of a more informal kind, e.g., through economic pressure, should be acceptable as long as the pressure remains within the prevailing legal structure.

Control by the majority.—It would seem to be unquestionable that the majority has the right of control and censorship. The question seems to be the possibility and feasibility of determining a majority in our pluralistic society. If and when this is done, general censorship laws are not only valid but needed.

Postal regulations against obscene and pornographic materials are an example of control by the majority. This is a general control law that was established for the protection of the majority against the malicious designs of the minority who would corrupt the morals and minds of individuals in society. Again, it must be said that such regulations are not a curb on freedom, but are to protect the freedom of the majority of the people who do not desire to have such materials sent through the mails.

Opponents of censorship in the field of mass communication would give the impression that any attempt at control is foreign to the American way of life. They hold that a man must be free to produce and distribute materials according to his desires, and that, through the process of education, the public itself can exercise self-censorship. They do not seem to understand that education itself has certain rules and laws which if not followed will result in anarchy. Freedom always carries responsibility. In a pluralistic society, if responsibilities are not maintained by an individual or group of individuals, their freedom must be limited out of regard for the freedom of others.

Therefore, certain principles need to be set out with regard to control by majority groups. How much control can be exercised? What regard must be given to minority groups?

1. Within a pluralist society the majority not only has the right but the responsibility to make whatever laws are necessary to protect not only themselves but the minority from materials considered harmful according to standards set out by the majority.

2. In a pluralist society the majority has the responsibility to

respect the desires and wishes of the minority as long as the minority remains within the legal structure set out by the majority.

3. This means that no minority, however vocal, has the right to force its views on the majority. At the same time, it means that any minority has the right to express its views unless those views would cause antisocial action within society.

4. In a pluralist society no minority group has the right or privilege to distribute, even by peaceful and legal means, materials which are deemed obscene or subversive by the majority.

Thus, unlimited control is not given into the hands of the majority. At the same time, the majority has the responsibility, being in the majority, to establish necessary controls for the protection of society. When this privilege is taken from the majority, democracy will begin to fail. Expression of ideas is essential to social growth and progress, but limitations and responsibility make up a price that must be paid for democracy.

Conclusion

The current picture for the proponents and opponents of censorship seems to be a cloudy and muddled affair. On the one hand, Zechariah Chafee, Jr., a man who is said to be one of this country's most distinguished defenders of constitutional freedom, said in 1944 that "liberties of speech, press, and assembly which were universally cherished in my boyhood have been eroded during the past 40 years by law after law, and only scattered protests have been heard." [29]

The situation is so bad, seemingly, that Stuart Sherman, librarian at Providence Public Library in New Jersey, says, "It was stated with some authority recently that if the Bill of Rights were put to a vote today in Congress there is reason to doubt that it would pass." [30]

On the other hand, the editor of *Saturday Evening Post* has said that "dozens of novels are published each year, any one of which, a few decades ago, would have sent publisher and writer to jail." [31] A cursory glance at any index system will show that more articles are being written on the problem today than ever before. Either the problem of obscenity and subversive materials is greater today or

---

[29] Stuart C. Sherman, "Defending the Freedom to Read," *Library Journal*, LXXXVII (February 1, 1962), 479.

[30] *Ibid.*

[31] "After Obscenity, What?" *op. cit.*, p. 80.

there is more awareness of the problem among the constituency of our population.

The problem of control will not be solved by simply delineating certain principles or techniques. Each situation will, no doubt, require a different answer. Because control will be difficult, however, does not mean that the answer is no control. In no other area of contemporary life in America is freedom allowed without a certain amount of responsibility. For those who would be irresponsible, control is necessary. Control in the area of mass communication will be not to limit freedom but to extend the freedom of the majority who do not want their minds nor the minds of their young people to become enslaved to passionate desires that are presented as normal realities. As Mr. Osmond K. Fraenkel, general counsel of the American Civil Liberties Union, has pointed out, "The battle for artistic freedom has been won." Therefore, he suggests that it might be well to "concentrate on laws designed to prevent distribution of pornography to the young." [32]

Rev. Robert F. Drinan, S.J., dean of the Boston College Law School, has warned against being deceived by those who would loudly declare that reading obscenity is a sort of "safety valve" for certain maladjusted persons. These people hold that some who would otherwise commit sex crimes might be saved from doing so if they could only give vent to their feelings by reading and "devouring" pornography. Father Drinan points out that obscenity is not only valueless, it is an offense against human dignity and decency.

One thing is certain, the publishers of filthy books and magazines know that sex sells, and that sex means money. The only limit they will observe is what one has called the "saturation point"—the amount of filth any particular community will tolerate. Therefore, the Christian community should become alert to the need for more support of whatever legal means can be established for the control of the sale and distribution of this objectionable material.

The failure in the past has been the inadequate definition of the responsibility of the Christian community. There can be no laws to regulate the *production* of this sort of material, or those who champion freedom and rights will have a legitimate complaint. However, no one will be able to protest the right of a community to

---

[32] Sheerin, *op. cit.*, p. 136.

restrict the *sale* and *distribution* of such material for the sake of a greater freedom—the freedom of people who have become addicted to pornography. Therefore, the Christian community should insist that "rights to protection against the indiscriminate sale and display of this material are at least as important and valid as the 'rights' of unscrupulous publishers who are unwilling to give up a lucrative business built upon the unwholesome aspects of sex and its perversion." [33]

Censorship, defined in this way, is positive—not negative. It is not *denying* rights and freedom but rather *protecting* rights and freedom through the medium of control.

Additional Reading

GARDINER, HAROLD CHARLES. *Catholic Viewpoint on Censorship.* Garden City, N. Y.: Doubleday & Co., 1958.

McKEON, RICHARD, *et al., The Freedom to Read.* New York: R. R. Bowker Co., 1957.

---

[33] Foster, *op. cit.,* p. 23.

Contributors

D. YATES BINGHAM, Air Force chaplain, is a native of North Carolina. He holds the B.A. degree from Wake Forest College and the B.D. and Th.D. degrees from Southwestern Baptist Theological Seminary. He served as pastor of churches in Texas, South Carolina, and North Carolina prior to his chaplaincy appointment, which he received in 1951. Major Bingham has served at Randolph Air Force Base, Texas; Tinker Air Force Base, Oklahoma; Ranstein Air Base in Germany; and Air Force bases in the Far East.

JULIAN C. BRIDGES, missionary in Mexico, is a native of Florida. He holds the B.A. degree from the University of Florida and the B.D. and Th.D. degrees from Southwestern Seminary. Prior to his appointment in 1960, by the Foreign Mission Board, as a Southern Baptist missionary to Mexico, Dr. Bridges served as pastor of churches in Texas for six years. Dr. and Mrs. Bridges reside in Mexico City, where he serves as director of the Student Department of the National Baptist Convention and as local director for the University Student Center and the University Student Home.

F. B. HUEY, Southern Baptist missionary in Brazil, is a Texas native. He holds the Bachelor of Business Administration from the University of Texas and the B.D. and Th.D. degrees from Southwestern Seminary. Before missionary appointment, Dr. Huey was pastor of the University Baptist Church, Denton, Texas. He serves now as professor of Old Testament and Hebrew at the South Brazil Baptist Theological Seminary in Rio de Janeiro.

W. RANDALL LOLLEY, pastor, First Baptist Church, Winston-Salem, North Carolina, is a native of Alabama. He holds the B.A. degree from Howard College, the B.D. and Th.M. degrees from Southeastern Baptist Theological Seminary, and the Th.D. degree from Southwestern Baptist Theological Seminary. Before going to his present pastorate, he served as associate pastor of Broadway Baptist Church, Fort Worth, Texas.

BILL PINSON, assistant professor of Christian ethics, Southwestern Baptist Theological Seminary, is a native of Texas. He holds the B.A. degree from North Texas State University, the B.D. and Th.D. degrees from Southwestern Seminary, and has studied at the University of Edinburg, Scotland. Dr. Pinson served for seven years as associate secretary of the Christian Life Commission, Baptist General Convention of Texas, before going to his present position.

P. EDWARD RICKENBAKER, pastor, First Baptist Church, Denmark, South Carolina, is a native of South Carolina. He holds the B.A. degree from Baylor University and the B.D. and Th.D. degrees from Southwestern Seminary. He has studied at the University of Miami, the University of South Carolina, and Wheaton College. Dr. Rickenbaker served as pastor of churches in Texas before going to his present pastorate.

JAMES M. ROBINSON, pastor, First Baptist Church, Sweetwater, Texas, is a native Texan. He holds the B.S. degree from Hardin-Simmons University and the B.D. and Th.D. degrees from Southwestern Seminary. Dr. Robinson has held pastorates in Texas for the past twelve years.

STANLEY O. WHITE, pastor, First Baptist Church, Weatherford, Texas, is a native of California. He holds the B.A. degree from Baylor and the B.D. degree from Southwestern Seminary, where he is a candidate for the Th.D. degree. He serves as a member of the Executive Board of the Baptist General Convention of Texas. He participated in the Japan Baptist New Life Movement of 1963, preaching in Honolulu, Hawaii; Kyoto, Japan; and Bangkok, Thailand.

G. RAY WORLEY, associate director, Seminary Extension Department of Southern Baptist Seminaries, is a native of Virginia. He holds the B.D. and Th.D. degrees from Southwestern Seminary. He has studied at Indiana University and Southern Baptist Theological Seminary. Prior to his present position, Dr. Worley served as chaplain and counselor at the Gatesville State School for Boys in Texas.